Better Homes & Gardens.

CHRISTMAS
FROM THE HEART.

Volume 27

Meredith. Consumer Marketing
Des Moines, Iowa

CHRISTMAS
FROM THE HEART.

MEREDITH CORPORATION CONSUMER MARKETING
Director of Direct Marketing-Books: Daniel Fagan
Marketing Operations Manager: Max Daily
Assistant Marketing Manager: Kylie Dazzo
Business Manager: Diane Umland
Senior Production Manager: Al Rodruck

WATERBURY PUBLICATIONS, INC.
Contributing Editor: Carol Field Dahlstrom
Contributing Copy Editor: Terri Fredrickson
Contributing Proofreader: Gretchen Kauffman
Contributing Photographer: Jacob Fox

Editorial Director: Lisa Kingsley
Creative Director: Ken Carlson
Associate Editor: Tricia Bergman
Associate Design Director: Doug Samuelson
Production Assistant: Mindy Samuelson

BETTER HOMES & GARDENS MAGAZINE
Editor in Chief: Stephen Orr
Executive Editor: Oma Blaise Ford
Managing Editor: Gregory H. Kayko
Creative Director: Jennifer D. Madara
Senior Deputy Editor, Food and Entertaining: Nancy Wall Hopkins

MEREDITH NATIONAL MEDIA GROUP
President and CEO: Tom Harty

MEREDITH CORPORATION
Executive Chairman: Stephen M. Lacy

In Memoriam: E.T. Meredith III (1933–2003)

All of us at Meredith Consumer Marketing are dedicated to
providing you with information and ideas to enhance your home.
We welcome your comments and suggestions. Write to us at:
Meredith Consumer Marketing, 1716 Locust St., Des Moines, IA 50309-3023.

Contents

PERFECTLY CHARMING

The happiest time of year is upon us, and we are here to share a multitude of ideas to help make this the best Christmas ever! We will show you how to create one-of-a-kind Christmas trees, deck the halls with on-trend accents, design your own fresh wreaths and swags, and make your own unique, handcrafted gifts, wraps, and cards.

Everyone loves Christmas cookies, and you'll be dazzled with our Almond Wreaths, Coconut Spritz, Chocolate Crinkles, and more! Make plenty to give and enough to enjoy with that Christmas Eve cup of hot chocolate. If you love entertaining, you'll be inspired with our amazing array of beautiful cheese boards to suit any holiday gathering.

You'll also find charming ideas to make your home into a farmhouse-style Christmas with projects like Clusters-of-Cotton Garland, Linen-Wrapped Ornaments, and Tin-Can Candles. Love the look of red and white? We'll show you how to make a candy cane wreath, a Candy Twist quilted table mat, and a Peppermint Candy Cookie Tray. In our chapter "Everything Evergreen," learn how to combine wispy and berried greenery into lovely wreaths, garlands, and swags for your holiday home. Need some great gift ideas? Try your hand at making a Reversible Snuggle Scarf or a Prancing Reindeer Pillow—then wrap them with the clever wraps and gift toppers that we show you how to make. You'll love our adorable gnomes made from pinecones and our all-in-white sparkling luminarias. And the place settings we share will make your holiday table sparkle.

We hope you are inspired, enthused, and excited to make this holiday full of charm and style as you create the perfect Christmas from the Heart.

Merry Christmas!

Carol Field Dahlstrom

Charming Farmhouse Christmas

Warm, earthy hues and plenty of natural textures set the stage for a festive on-trend farmhouse style with a nod to the great outdoors.

HEARTFELT HOLDERS

Stamp and share your holiday message onto a snippet of wood and display it on simple farmhouse-style wood post holders.

WHAT YOU NEED

Wood posts cut into 5- to 10-inch heights • White chalk paint • Paintbrush • Sandpaper • Saw • Bakers twine • Natural found objects such as acorns, pods, greenery • Balsa wood • Scissors • Brown paint • Stamp and ink pad

WHAT YOU DO

1. Paint posts with white chalk paint. Let dry. Distress with sandpaper.
2. Use a saw to cut a slit into the top of the post about 1 inch deep and ¼ inch wide.
3. Use twine to wrap around the middle of each piece, adding natural found objects to each post piece.
4. To make the wood message toppers, use scissors or a knife to cut thin balsa wood into pieces slightly longer than the diameter of the post pieces. Paint the pieces brown. Let dry. Distress with sandpaper.
5. Stamp a message or phrase onto the painted pieces; place a message piece into the slot on top of each post.

PAILS OF PLENTY

Toss-away tin cans take on new life with a little paint spatter, twine bails, and favorite holiday goodies.

WHAT YOU NEED

Tin vegetable cans, washed and dried • Spray paint in desired colors • Acrylic paint in desired colors • Paintbrush • Drill and metal drill bit • Small pieces of birch • Twine • Scissors • Tissue paper • Candy canes, wrapped candies, caramel corn

WHAT YOU DO

1. Lay the tin cans on a covered surface and spray with a dusting of spray paint. Using a paintbrush, spatter the acrylic paint on top of the spray paint. Let dry.
2. Drill a hole in each side of the can large enough for the twine. Cut the birch branch into about 2-inch pieces. Drill a hole in the ends of the birch pieces and thread a piece of twine into the hole, making the bail for the can.
3. Thread the twine from the inside to the outside through the hole in the can. Tie a knot to secure with the knot on the outside.
4. Tuck tissue paper in the cans and fill with candy canes, wrapped candies, or caramel corn.

KRAFT PAPER COZY

Plain brown paper is tied up with strings and tucked around a large tin can to create a simple holder for a fresh evergreen tree.

WHAT YOU NEED

Large vegetable tin can, washed and dried • Brown kraft paper • Scissors • Large needle • String • Wooden die-cut ornament • Evergreen tree • Ornaments to decorate tree • Small stones or sand

WHAT YOU DO

1. Be sure the can is clean and dry. Cut a piece of kraft paper large enough to fit around the can. Position the can in the center of the paper, bring the paper up and around the tin, and tuck it around the top.

2. Thread the needle with the string and use a long decorative running stitch around the top of the paper, weaving the string in and out. Leave tails of string at the front of the can.

3. Tie the ornament onto the tails of the string. Place the tree into the can and secure with stones or sand. Decorate the tree as desired.

COZY FARMHOUSE FIREPLACE

A reproduction weathered barn door adorned with a purchased cotton-ball wreath creates the perfect farmhouse-style backdrop above the mantel, while woven baskets and giant pinecones lend rustic texture among fresh evergreen boughs. Tiny tree toppers in terra-cotta pots balance on the mantel that features Subtle Plaid Stockings and Clusters of Cotton Garland.

CLUSTERS OF COTTON GARLAND

Cotton-ball picks combine with natural pinecones to make a holiday garland for mantel or banister.

WHAT YOU NEED

7 to 10 stems of cotton ball picks (available at crafts stores or online) • PInecones • Wire • Wire cutters

WHAT YOU DO

1. Lay out the cotton-ball picks to decide the desired length. Wire and twist the picks together.
2. Cut the wire into 8-inch pieces and wire the pinecones onto the garland. Trim the ends if needed.

SUBTLE PLAID STOCKINGS

Even if you don't live in a real farmhouse, these stockings made from linenlike fabric hanging on the mantel will make your home feel like a country Christmas.

WHAT YOU NEED (FOR ONE STOCKING)
½ yard plaid fabric • Scissors• ¼ yard solid linen or linenlike fabric • Sewing machine • Needle and thread to match fabrics

WHAT YOU DO
1. Enlarge and copy the pattern, right. Cut out.
2. Fold plaid fabric in half, right sides together, then trace stocking pattern on fabric and cut out through both layers. Fold solid fabric in half, right sides together, then trace cuff on fabric and cut out through both layers. Fray along bottom edge of each cuff by pulling threads from fabric.
3. With right sides together and ½-inch seam allowance, stitch long sides of solid fabric together, creating a tube. Insert nonfrayed end of tube into stocking and stitch top edge of stocking to tube. Turn the frayed end right side out, pulling it down over the top of the stocking to fashion the cuff. Press, then hand-stitch a fabric loop inside top opening for hanging.

Subtle Plaid Stocking Pattern
Enlarge 200%

Rustic touches from the outdoors combine with handmade trims to usher the Christmas spirit into your farmhouse-style home. Foam balls are wrapped with linen strips, and a thick twine cord becomes a simple garland for a tree nestled into a stump of wood.

NATURAL ELEMENTS

A fresh evergreen rests in a rustic tree stump for a friendly, farmhouse look. The stump is drilled in the middle, and the bottom of the tree is pared down to fit tightly. Linen-Wrapped Ornaments and a Stick Star Topper adorn the tree.

LINEN-WRAPPED ORNAMENTS

Strips of torn fabric wrap around foam balls to create natural-looking ornaments for your farmhouse tree.

WHAT YOU NEED

Linen or linenlike fabric • Foam balls such as Styrofoam • Scissors • Straight pins • Charms and jewelry loop findings • Hot-glue gun and glue sticks • Bakers twine

WHAT YOU DO

1. Tear or cut the linen into ½- to 1-inch strips. Starting at the top of the ball, pin the strip to secure. Wrap around the ball until it is covered.

2. Create a hanger for the ball by gluing a jewelry hook to a round charm. Let dry. Glue to the top of the ball. Let dry.

3. Thread the twine through the top of the ball for hanging.

STICK STAR TOPPER

Simple sticks or small branches crisscross to make a perfect star topper for your rustic tree.

WHAT YOU NEED

Small sticks or branches cut into 7- to 8-inch lengths • Hot-glue gun and glue sticks • Copper wire • Wire cutters

WHAT YOU DO

1. Lay the sticks atop each other to form a star. Be sure that the branches touch each other so they can be easily glued and wired together.

2. Use dots of glue to secure in place. Let dry.

3. Cut the copper wire into pieces and wrap around the ends and middle to secure. Trim the ends.

VILLAGE CANDLES

Scraps of wood combine with little pieces of felt to become a village of candleholders for your holiday table or mantel.

WHAT YOU NEED
Wood remnants at least 2 inches thick • Saw • Drill and drill bit to fit candle size • Painters tape • Craft paint • Paintbrush • Felt • Scissors • Hot-glue gun and glue sticks • Candles

WHAT YOU DO
1. Lay out the wood pieces and plan the design by cutting off the top of the wood at angles to resemble roofs.
2. Drill straight down through the top of the roof shape.
3. Use painters tape to mark off areas of the house to be painted. Paint the houses using craft paint. Let dry.
4. Embellish with doors and windows created from felt. Attach with hot glue.
5. Place candles in the houses.

Never leave a burning candle unattended.

TIN-CAN CANDLES

Tiny tin cans line up together to make perfect holders for holiday votives.

WHAT YOU NEED

5 small tin cans such as 8-oz. vegetable cans ● Bakers twine ● Scissors ● 5 glass votive holders and candles

WHAT YOU DO

1. Be sure the cans are clean and dry.
2. Line up the cans in a row. Starting with the first can, loop the twine around the cans in and out. Continue until the cans are secure. Tie at the end.
3. Set the votive holders and candles in the cans.

Never leave a burning candle unattended.

CAST-IRON CANDLES

Small-size cast-iron pans become cozy candles in any color that fits your decorating style.

WHAT YOU NEED

Small-size cast-iron frying pan • Candle wicking • Pencils • Scissors • Old candles or candle wax in desired colors • Old can for melting wax • Old sauce pan to hold the can of wax • Hot plate or stove

WHAT YOU DO

1. Be sure the cast-iron pans are clean and dry. If new, wipe out with soft cloth. Cut three pieces of candle wicking and wrap one end around a pencil, leaving the other end to extend into the pan for the wick. (See photo at right.) Set aside

2. Chunk the wax or old candles into the old can. Set the can into the saucepan. Fill the saucepan with water until it comes up about 3 inches on the can. Heat on the stove or hot plate on medium heat until the wax is just melted.

Caution: DO NOT overheat. Wax can heat up fast and explode if overheated.

3. Carefully pour the melted wax into the prepared pans. Let set until firm. Remove pencils and trim wicks.

Never leave a burning candle unattended.

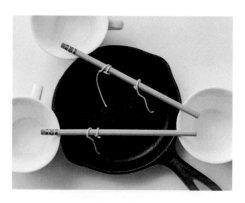

ORNAMENTAL COUNTDOWN

A mishmash of old and new ornaments marks the days on this Advent calendar. To create the calendar, adhere number stickers to shopping tags, then use gold straight pins to attach the tags and a collection of shapely ornaments to an artist's canvas backed with foam-core board.

TAG IT HOLIDAY LADDER

Dress up seed-starter peat pots with acrylic paints and glued-on colorful felt and fabric trims. Create numbered tags, hot-gluing a button to each tag and the tags to pots. Using a large needle and twine, create a hanger for each pot and tie each to a vintage ladder or other display. Fill each pot with signs of the season—peppermint sticks, candy canes, gingerbread shapes, and more.

CHALK IT UP MESSAGES

WHAT YOU NEED

Practice paper • Round kraft paper ornaments • Charcoal chalk paint • Paintbrush • White chalk marker

WHAT YOU DO

1. Plan the design of the ornament by using chalk to practice making words and shapes on practice paper.
2. Paint the ornaments using a paintbrush. Let dry.
3. Use the chalk marker to draw designs on the ornaments.

WOODLAND TREE

Dress up a country tree topper with Oatmeal Ornaments and packages wrapped in brown paper wrap. Place the tree in a tin pail and surround it with simple packages. The brown paper wrap is embellished with Christmas words written with permanent marker and tied up with twine.

Rustic and full of earthy texture, these ornaments are made using simple ingredients from your kitchen. Choose cookie cutters to make the shapes or hand cut the pieces using a knife. Use twine to hang the trims on a fresh evergreen tree for a farmhouse look.

OATMEAL ORNAMENTS

Use humble ingredients to create something beautiful for your holiday decorating.

WHAT YOU NEED

Baking sheet • Parchment paper • 3 cups flour • 1 cup salt • 1 cup quick oatmeal • 1 cup warm water • Rolling pin • Knife • Cookie or biscuit cutters: round, hearts, stars • Bamboo skewer • Twine for hangers

WHAT YOU DO

1. Preheat oven to 200°F. Cover baking sheet with parchment paper. Set aside.

2. In a large bowl combine flour, salt, and oatmeal. Pour in the warm water and mix with your hands to form dough. Knead the dough until it is smooth and uniform in color.

3. Using a rolling pin, roll dough to ⅛-inch thickness. Cut circles, hearts, squares, and stars from dough using a knife, cookie cutters, or biscuit cutters. Sprinkle with more oatmeal on top and press in place. Place shapes on prepared baking sheet. Poke a hole through each shape using a bamboo skewer.

4. Bake 2 to 3 hours or until shapes are completely hard.

Note: Test the hardness by tapping the shapes with your fingernail. If they sound hollow, remove them from the oven. Let cool completely.

5. Thread twine through each hole for hanging.

Note: These ornaments should not be eaten. Ornaments are for decoration only.

The Big Cheese

What's a party without cheese? First, master the cheese board. Then, if your friends are true cheese fiends, step up your game with cheesecentric appetizers and snacks.

MEET THE CHEESES

We've merely scraped the rind of the vast world of cheese with these easy-to-find, crowd-pleasing varieties. Flavors, textures, and best uses vary based on the type of milk, add-ins, aging processes, and more.

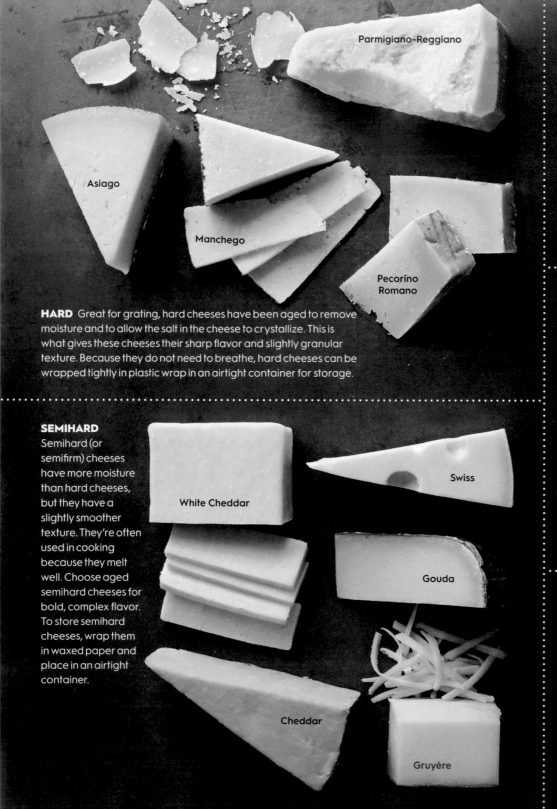

Parmigiano-Reggiano

Asiago

Manchego

Pecorino Romano

HARD Great for grating, hard cheeses have been aged to remove moisture and to allow the salt in the cheese to crystallize. This is what gives these cheeses their sharp flavor and slightly granular texture. Because they do not need to breathe, hard cheeses can be wrapped tightly in plastic wrap in an airtight container for storage.

SEMIHARD
Semihard (or semifirm) cheeses have more moisture than hard cheeses, but they have a slightly smoother texture. They're often used in cooking because they melt well. Choose aged semihard cheeses for bold, complex flavor. To store semihard cheeses, wrap them in waxed paper and place in an airtight container.

White Cheddar

Swiss

Gouda

Cheddar

Gruyère

SEMISOFT Semisoft cheeses have lots of moisture, and their texture makes them easy to slice and tuck into cold sandwiches. To store semisoft cheeses, wrap in waxed paper and place in an airtight container.

Ask for Help: Talk to a cheesemonger at a cheese shop or in a supermarket with trained staff. They can teach you about types of cheeses and the regions where they are produced. You'll be able to sample a variety and ask questions about the best ways to enjoy each cheese.

BLUE Blue cheeses contain blue veins created by the addition of mold during the cheese-making process. Softer blue cheeses can be used for spreading and melt well in cooking. Slice and serve higher-end, drier blues for snacking, sandwiches, and cheese boards. Wrap blue cheeses in foil or waxed paper, then in plastic wrap.

FRESH Fresh, unaged cheeses have a high moisture content, soft texture, and flavors that range from mild to tangy. Store, tightly covered, in their original containers (and original liquid if applicable) up to 5 days.

Ricotta

Mascarpone

Fresh mozzarella

Fontina

Monterey Jack

Muenster

Havarti

SOFT-RIPENED Soft-ripened cheeses have a smooth interior and a thin, bloomy rind. Brie and Camembert have similar flavors and can be used interchangeably in recipes. However, Camembert typically has a slightly stronger flavor and firmer texture than Brie. Store soft-ripened cheeses wrapped in waxed paper, which allows them to breathe.

Camembert

Brie

Feta

Blue cheese

Gorgonzola

Roquefort

Stilton

Chèvre

CHEESE-LOVER'S BOARD

A basic cheese board should be a mix of cow's, sheep's, and goat's milk cheeses; aged and fresh cheeses; and salty, subtly sweet, funky, and mild flavors. Keep add-ons easy and let the cheeses steal the show. Allow cheese to mellow at room temperature for about an hour before serving: Flavors will be muted if the cheese is too cold.

1. Soft-Ripened: Brie
A cow's milk cheese with a smooth, soft texture.

2. Blue: American
A creamy, crumbly, and smooth cow's milk cheese with a mellow, almost sweet flavor.

3. Fresh: Whipped Feta
A spreadable blend of sheep's milk cheese (see recipe below).

4. Hard: Parmesan
A crumbly, grainy cow's milk cheese with a sharp, nutty flavor.

5. Semihard: Aged Cheddar
Crumbly with a sharp, salty, subtly sweet flavor.

6. Semisoft: Havarti
A fresh cow's milk cheese with a smooth, buttery flavor.

7. Fresh: Goat Cheese
Sweet and mellow with tangy, nutty notes and a crumbly texture.

Whipped Feta In a food processor pulse 1 clove garlic until finely chopped. Add 1 tsp. lemon zest, 1 Tbsp. lemon juice, 1½ cups crumbled feta cheese, and 2 oz. softened cream cheese. Process until smooth. Add 2 Tbsp. extra virgin olive oil; process until light and fluffy. Season to taste with freshly ground black pepper.

The Extras
Grapes, Fruit preserves, Marcona almonds, Honey, Crackers, Baguette slices

CARNIVORE BOARD

Bold, strongly flavored cheeses can stand up to the rich, salty, umami flavors of cured meats, tangy whole grain mustard, and pickled veggies. Semihard, semisoft, and fresh cheese textures play well with crunchy crackers and baguette slices—think of each bite of bread, meat, and cheese as a mini sandwich.

The Extras
Marinated artichokes, Whole-grain mustard, Antipasto, Crackers, Baguette slices, Prosciutto, Soppresata, Calabrese, Capicola

1. Fresh: Ash-Ripened Goat Cheese	2. Blue: Stilton	3. Semihard: Manchego	4. Semihard: White Cheddar	5. Fresh: Mozzarella with Charcuterie
Ash applied during aging imparts smoky, grassy flavor.	A spicy English-style blue with a semisoft creamy, crumbly texture.	A Spanish sheep's milk cheese with a nutty, rich, mellow flavor.	A cow's milk cheese with a salty, super-savory flavor.	Cured meat-wrapped fresh cheese is easy to DIY!

PICKLED BOARD

Creamy, mild cheeses let pickled accessories—kimchi, pickled veggies, briny olives—pop, while salty, aged cheeses mirror the tang of pleasantly fermented add-ons. Use small bowls and dishes to add structure and keep liquidy sides from watering down their neighbors.

The Extras: Sauerkraut, Kimchi, Pickled veggies, Pickles, Marinated olives, Crispy breadsticks

1. Semihard: Sharp Cheddar
Buttery and grassy with a flavor that's equal parts salty and sweet.

2. Fresh: Mozzarella
A creamy, milky, tender cow's milk cheese with mild flavor.

3. Soft-Ripened: Triple Cream
A mild, spreadable, super-rich cheese thanks to added cream.

4. Blue: Maytag
A semihard blue with a crumbly texture and strong, tangy flavor.

5. Semihard: Comté
A dense, slightly grainy cheese with a salty, nutty, toasty flavor.

DESSERT BOARD

No need to pigeonhole a cheese board as an appetizer. Some cheese textures, flavors, and milk sources lend themselves to sweet pairings: Match young (unaged), fruity, and subtly sweet cheeses with fruit, chocolate, and other sweet board toppers. After you anchor the board with cheese and small dishes, fill any gaps with loose piles of dried fruit, nuts, and fresh herbs.

1. Fresh: Wine-Soaked Goat Cheese
A smooth, semifirm cheese with fruity notes (compliments of the wine).

2. Fresh: Chèvre
Fresh and rindless with a soft, smooth texture. Try it with finely chopped dried fruit and rosemary.

3. Soft-Ripened: Brie
A buttery, nutty, soft, and fruity cow's milk cheese.

4. Fresh: Ricotta
Fresh cheese with a smooth, spreadable texture and a delicate, milky flavor.

The Extras: Fresh fruit, Dried fruit, Quince paste, Honeycomb, Caramel corn, Chocolate, Toast

RACLETTE

There's Swiss cheese for a sandwich and then there's the kind of Swiss cheese that brings the party. Raclette—a cow's milk cheese with a semisoft texture and pungent, full flavor—takes its name from the French verb racler, *which means "to scrape." Heat raclette to a melt and scrape onto breads, veggies, and cured meats (or use those as dippers for the cheese).*

WHAT YOU NEED

3   to 4 lb. raclette, Fontina, and/or Emmental cheese wedges, rind removed

1   1-lb. loaf crusty bread
    Dippers, such as boiled baby yellow potatoes, steamed broccoli, cauliflower, and Brussels sprouts; sautéed asparagus, button mushrooms, or sweet peppers; thinly sliced salami or prosciutto

WHAT YOU DO

1. Heat an 8- to 10-inch cast-iron skillet over medium. Add cheese; cook 2 to 4 minutes or until cheese starts to melt, turning once. Continue cooking and turning until cheese is softened but still slightly firm in center. (Use a ventilation fan while heating; the melting cheese creates a pungent aroma.)
2. Serve melty cheese with crusty bread and dippers. Makes 8 servings.

SMOKY CHEESE BALL

This party-perfect make-ahead appetizer never goes out of style—and you can customize it with the type of cheese and nuts you choose.

WHAT YOU NEED

2   8-oz. pkg. cream cheese

2   cups finely shredded smoked cheddar, Swiss, or Gouda cheese

½   cup butter or margarine

2   Tbsp. milk

2   tsp. steak sauce

1   cup finely chopped toasted nuts
    Assorted crackers

WHAT YOU DO

1. In a medium bowl combine first five ingredients (through steak sauce). Beat with a mixer on medium to high until fluffy, scraping bowl as needed. Cover and chill 4 to 24 hours.
2. Shape cheese mixture into a ball; roll in nuts. Let stand 15 minutes before serving. Serve with crackers. Makes 56 servings (1 Tbsp. each).
To Make Ahead Prepare as directed, except do not roll in nuts. Wrap cheese ball in moistureproof/vaporproof plastic wrap. Freeze up to 1 month. To serve, thaw cheese ball in refrigerator overnight. Roll in nuts. Let stand 30 minutes at room temperature before serving.

2. Spread jelly over top of each cheese round. Sprinkle with nuts; lightly press nuts into jelly.

3. Combine egg and the water. Place pastry circles over cheese rounds; invert rounds and pastry. Lightly brush edges of pastry with egg mixture. Bring pastry up and over cheese rounds, pleating and pinching edges to cover and seal. Trim excess pastry. Place rounds, smooth sides up, on prepared baking sheet. Brush tops and sides with egg mixture. Cut small slits for steam to escape. Using hors d'oeuvre cutters, cut shapes from pastry trimmings. Brush shapes with egg mixture; place on top of rounds.

4. Bake 20 to 25 minutes or until pastry is deep golden brown. Let stand 10 to 20 minutes before serving. If desired, serve with apple and/or pear slices. Makes 12 servings (¾ oz. each).

Tip To toast nuts, spread evenly in a shallow pan and bake in a 350°F oven 5 to 10 minutes, stirring once or twice (and watching closely). Or toast finely chopped nuts in a dry skillet over medium, stirring often.

BEER-CHEESE FONDUE

No fondue pot? No problem. This fondue is made—and kept warm—in a slow cooker.

WHAT YOU NEED

1½   cups reduced-sodium chicken broth
1¼   cups heavy cream
½   cup lager beer
2   cloves garlic, minced
½   cup butter, softened
½   cup all-purpose flour
1½   tsp. spicy brown mustard
2   cups shredded mild cheddar cheese (8 oz.)
1   cup shredded sharp cheddar cheese (4 oz.)
      Assorted dippers, such as French bread cubes, soft pretzels, vegetable sticks, steamed broccoli florets, boiled potatoes, and/or cooked shaped pasta

WHAT YOU DO

1. In a 1½- or 2-qt. slow cooker combine first four ingredients (through garlic). Cover and cook on low 4 to 5 hours. Meanwhile, in a bowl stir together butter and flour until a paste forms.

2. Turn cooker to high. Whisk paste into broth mixture until smooth (mixture will thicken immediately). Cover; cook 30 minutes more.

3. Whisk mustard into broth mixture. Gradually whisk in cheeses until smooth. Serve with dippers. Makes 22 servings (¼ cup each).

Stove Top Method To make on the stove top, in a medium saucepan melt butter over medium heat. Add garlic; cook and stir 2 minutes. Whisk in flour; cook and stir 1 minute. Gradually whisk in broth, cream, and beer. Cook and stir until thickened and bubbly. Whisk in mustard until smooth, then gradually whisk in cheeses until melted and smooth. If desired for serving, transfer fondue to a slow cooker set on warm.

BRIE EN CROÛTE

Slices of crisp and sweet apple and/or pear are a refreshing complement to this decadent gooey cheese baked in a pastry crust.

WHAT YOU NEED

½   of a 17.3-oz. pkg. (1 sheet) frozen puff pastry sheets, thawed
2   Tbsp. jalapeño, apple, or apricot jelly
2   4½-oz. rounds Brie or Camembert cheese
2   Tbsp. chopped nuts, toasted (tip, right)
1   egg, slightly beaten
1   Tbsp. water
      Apple and/or pear slices (optional)

WHAT YOU DO

1. Preheat oven to 400°F. Grease a baking sheet; set aside. Unfold pastry on a lightly floured surface; roll into a 16×10-inch rectangle. Cut into two 8-inch circles, reserving trimmings.

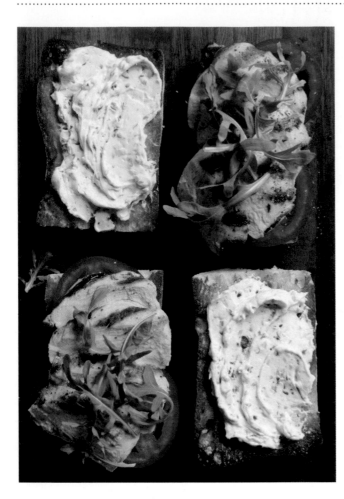

GOURNAY-STYLE CHEESE SPREAD

If you're familiar with Boursin, the processed, triple-cream cheese spread, you're familiar with Gournay-style cheese. Our version starts with cream cheese and incorporates herbs and aromatics, all whirred together in the food processor.

WHAT YOU NEED
½   cup packed fresh Italian parsley leaves
2   Tbsp. coarsely chopped green onion
1   clove garlic, halved
1   8-oz. pkg. cream cheese, softened
2   Tbsp. unsalted butter, softened
1   Tbsp. plain Greek yogurt (optional)
    Salt and freshly ground black pepper

WHAT YOU DO
1. In a food processor combine parsley, green onion, and garlic until finely chopped. Transfer to a bowl. In processor combine cream cheese, butter, and, if desired, yogurt; cover and process until smooth.
2. Return parsley mixture to processor; cover and pulse to combine. Season to taste with salt and pepper. Store in refrigerator until ready to use (up to 1 week). Makes 21 servings (1 Tbsp. each).

PIZZA MARGHERITA

Fresh mozzarella is prized for its mild, delicate flavor and smooth texture. Small mozzarella balls, also known as bocconcini or pearls, are perfect for topping pizzas. If you can only find large balls of fresh mozzarella, freeze a ball 15 minutes to firm it up, then cut it into smaller pieces.

WHAT YOU NEED
1   11-oz. pkg. refrigerated thin-crust pizza dough
1   Tbsp. olive oil
2   cups grape tomatoes, halved
8   oz. small fresh mozzarella cheese balls, sliced
2   cloves garlic, minced
½   cup fresh basil leaves
    Coarse-ground black pepper

WHAT YOU DO
1. Preheat oven to 400°F. Coat a 15×10-inch baking pan with nonstick cooking spray. Unroll pizza dough in prepared pan; press onto bottom and slightly up sides. Brush with oil. Bake 7 minutes.
2. Top with tomatoes, cheese, and garlic. Bake 8 to 10 minutes more or until crust is golden. Tear or snip large basil leaves. Sprinkle pizza with basil and pepper. Makes 6 servings (1 piece each).

CREAM CHEESE PASTRIES

Frozen puff pastry makes turning out bakery quality pastries a snap. Serve these as a sweet finishing touch.

WHAT YOU NEED

1½ cups fresh or frozen fruit, such as berries; sliced kumquats; chopped or thinly sliced apples, peaches, or pears; and/or pitted tart red or dark sweet cherries
1   8-oz. pkg. cream cheese, softened
⅓   cup sugar
1   tsp. lemon or lime juice
½   to 1 tsp. vanilla, almond, coffee, or lemon extract
½   cup preserves, jam, or marmalade
1   17.3-oz. pkg. (2 sheets) frozen puff pastry sheets, thawed
1   egg, lightly beaten
1   Tbsp. water

WHAT YOU DO

1. Thaw fruit if frozen. Preheat oven to 400°F. Line two large baking sheets with parchment paper.
2. In a medium bowl beat cream cheese with a mixer on medium until smooth. Add sugar, lemon juice, and vanilla; beat until combined. In a small bowl stir together fruit and preserves.
3. On a lightly floured surface roll one puff pastry sheet at a time into a 10½-inch square. (While you work, keep remaining sheet chilled so it doesn't get too soft.) Cut into nine 3½-inch squares; place on a prepared baking sheet. Prick with a fork to within ½ inch of the edges. Combine egg and the water; brush over squares. Spread each center with 1 Tbsp. cream cheese mixture; top with about 1½ Tbsp. fruit mixture.
4. Bake 15 to 18 minutes or until golden. Remove; cool on wire racks. Repeat with remaining puff pastry sheet. Makes 18 pastries.

Peppermint Pretty

With a touch of magically striped sweetness, candy canes always say "Merry Christmas."

Simple peppermint candy cane shapes become a delicate heart wreath when they are glued together and tied up with string. Hang the clever wreath in a window or make plenty and use as sweet tree ornaments.

HEART-TO-HEART CANDY CANE WREATH

WHAT YOU NEED

Twelve 7-inch candy canes • Two 4-inch candy canes • Hot-glue gun and glue sticks • Red cording • Scissors

WHAT YOU DO

1. Carefully unwrap the 12-inch candy canes and lay each set of two into a heart shape. Repeat to make six sets.

2. Using a tiny dot of hot glue, secure each set of candy canes at top and bottom.

3. With red cording tie the canes together at the curve of the heart formed by the canes.

4. Lay the cane sets together to form a wreath and use hot glue to secure.

5. Unwrap the smaller candy canes and lay on the center of the wreath to form a heart shape. Use small dots of hot glue to secure.

6. Loop the red cording through the top of the wreath for hanging.

Note: Candy canes should not be eaten after being used for crafting.

PEPPERMINT CANDY COOKIE TRAY

Your cookies will look even sweeter when you present them on a clever peppermint-candy cookie tray.

WHAT YOU NEED

13-inch white plate charger • Red felt • Scissors • Spray adhesive • Clear cellophane • String

WHAT YOU DO

1. Be sure the charger is clean and dry. Enlarge and copy the template, opposite. Using the template, cut 7 shapes from red felt.

2. Lay the pieces of felt on the charger in a spiral pattern. Attach the felt pieces to the charger with spray adhesive. Let dry.

3. Wrap the plate with cellophane, leaving excess at each end of charger. Tie string around each end to create the look of a candy wrapper.

Peppermint Candy Cookie Tray Template
Enlarge 150%
Cut 7

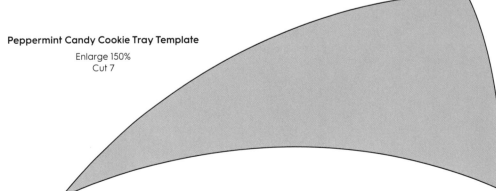

CANDY TWIST QUILTED TABLE RUNNER

Choose tiny-patterned fabric in red, pink, and white to make a perfectly peppermint table runner for your holiday table.

WHAT YOU NEED

Finished size: 13×33-inch
¼-inch seam allowances on 40-inch-wide fabric

1 yard white snowflake print for background, sashing, and backing • ½ yard red and white stripe for candy blocks and binding • 3 (¼-yard) red prints for candy blocks • 2 (¼-yard) pink prints for candy blocks • 16×36-inch piece batting

WHAT YOU DO

FROM WHITE SNOWFLAKE PRINT FABRIC CUT:

3—2½-inch-wide strips. Cut into 10 (9⅛×2½-inch) pieces for rectangle E. (page 44)
6—3⅜-inch squares. Cut each square in half diagonally to make 12 triangle C.
3 — Template A hexagons. (page 44)
1 — 16×36-inch backing

FROM RED AND WHITE STRIPE FABRIC CUT:

4—Template B triangles. (page 44) Place long side of triangle on one of the stripes and cut so each triangle is the same.
Enough 2-inch-wide bias strips to make 100 inches of binding.

FROM THE REMAINING RED PRINTS AND PINK PRINTS EACH CUT:

4—Template B triangles. If the print is directional, cut the triangles so each triangle is the same.

From one of the red prints cut:

8—2½-inch square D. (page 44)

ASSEMBLING THE QUILT CENTER

1. Select three groups of two coordinating triangles to make each candy twist block.
2. For each block, referring to Diagram 1, lay 1 triangle B on a hexagon A, matching at the hexagon corner. Sew a partial seam.
3. Working in a clockwise direction and referring to Diagram 2, add a coordinating fabric to the new long side and stitch. Continue adding the remaining 4 alternating fabric triangles. Complete the partial seam.
4. Referring to Diagram 3, add a white triangle C to 4 corners of the hexagon to complete 1 block. Make 3 blocks.
5. Referring to Quilt Top Assembly Diagram (page 44), arrange the 3 blocks, 8 squares D, and 10 rectangles E. Join into rows and join rows to make quilt top.

FINISHING

1. Layer the quilt top batting and backing.
2. Quilt as desired.
3. Trim the excess batting and backing.
4. Join the bias binding strips, fold in half, and use to bind quilt.

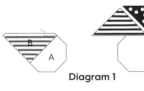

Diagram 1

Diagram 2

Diagram 3

Templates continue on page 44.

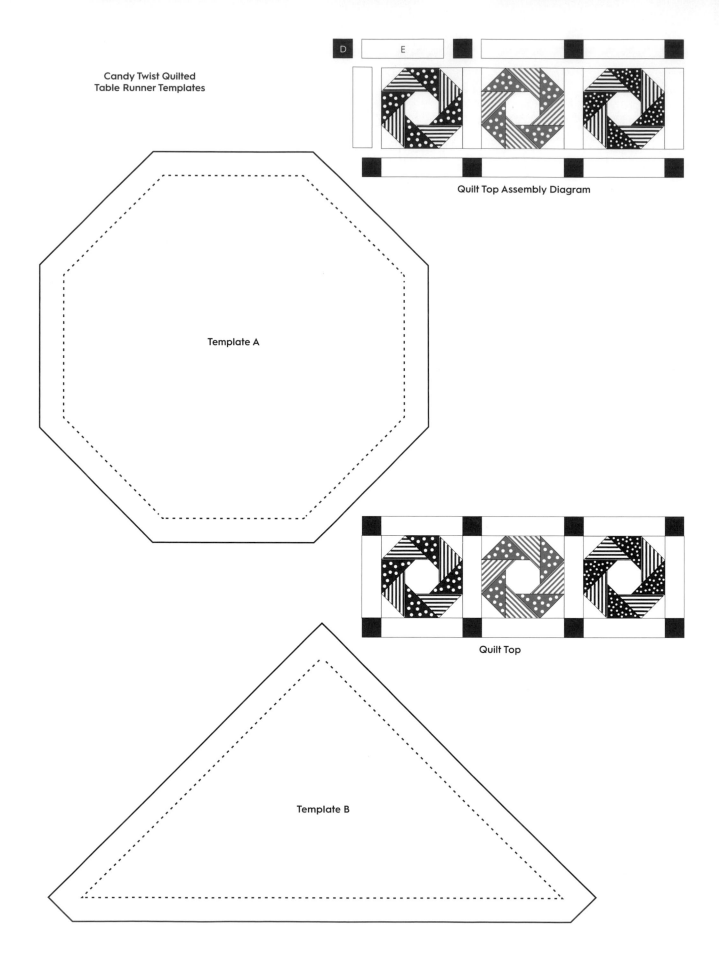

Candy Twist Quilted
Table Runner Templates

Quilt Top Assembly Diagram

Template A

Quilt Top

Template B

RICKRACK CANDY CANE BAGS

Scraps of rickrack are entwined to form candy canes to decorate felt gift bags for holiday giving.

WHAT YOU NEED

Red medium or jumbo rickrack • Foam block such as Styrofoam • Straight pins • Scissors • Crafts glue • Purchased or handmade gift bags • Needle and thread (optional) • Fabric glue (optional)

WHAT YOU DO

1. Decide on the approximate size of the candy cane. Cut a piece of red and white rickrack three times as long as the desired finished size.

2. Place the two pieces of rickrack together and tuck one piece of the rickrack inside the other. Pin flat to the foam block.

3. Continue to twist the rickrack together, pinning as you go to the foam block, and curving the pieces to form the shape. The rickrack should lie flat. Continue until the desired length is made. Remove from the foam block. Trim ends. Add a dot of crafts glue to each end to secure.

4. Make 2 other lengths of the twisted rickrack for the handles.

5. Use small stitches or fabric glue to attach the candy cane shapes to the fronts of the bags and the handles to the tops of the bags.

SOFT AND SWEET STITCHES

Soft wool pom-poms are embroidered and strung together for a festive handmade garland to drape on your tree or mantel.

WHAT YOU NEED

Wool pom-poms (See Sources, page 160) • Needle • Scissors • Red embroidery floss • Red-and-white striped bakers twine

WHAT YOU DO

1. Pinch the wool pom-pom with your fingers to flatten as flat as possible.
2. Thread the needle with three strands of embroidery floss. Using a straight stitch, create designs on the pom-pom, stitching around the perimeter or stitching through the center of the pom-pom to create the desired design.
3. Tie loose ends together on the back of the pom-pom. If desired, clip ends and secure with hot glue.
4. String the embroidered pom-poms together with needle and red-and-white bakers twine.

PLAYFUL POM-POM GARLAND

Candy canes form the sweet little hooks that secure this happy garland to your Christmas tree.

WHAT YOU NEED

Large red pom-poms • Large white pom-poms • Small red pom-poms • Red-and-white bakers twine • Needle large enough to thread twine • Scissors • Two 7-inch candy canes

WHAT YOU DO

1. Lay out the pom-poms in the order to be threaded.
2. Thread the needle with the bakers twine. Run the needle through the pom-poms in the order to be threaded. Tie a knot at each end.
3. Tie a candy cane at each end for hanging.

PAPER CANDY GARLAND

Tiny pieces of paper roll up to create a simple and sweet garland for your tree or mantel.

WHAT YOU NEED

Scissors • Patterned cardstock • Pencil or marker (optional) • Tape • Cellophane • Hot-glue gun and glue sticks • Needle • Red-and-white striped baker's twine

WHAT YOU DO

1. Cut cardstock into 1½×2-inch pieces. Form paper into a cylinder, securing with tape. **Tip:** Wrap the paper around a pencil or a marker to get a crisp shape.

2. Cut a 2×4-inch piece of cellophane. Roll around the paper cylinder. Twist ends of cellophane and secure with hot glue.

3. Thread the needle with bakers twine. String the paper candy pieces together.

SWEETLY-STRIPED CANDLEHOLDERS

Candy canes stand up to serve a pretty purpose when they combine to make holiday candleholders.

WHAT YOU NEED

Parchment paper or waxed paper • 12-inch candy canes • 4-inch candy canes • Rubber bands • Scissors • Taper candles • Hot-glue gun and glue sticks

WHAT YOU DO

1. Cover the working surface with parchment or waxed paper. Unwrap the candy canes. Carefully stand them up with the curved sides down around the taper candle. Temporarily secure with rubber bands.

2. Use hot glue to add small dots of glue between the candy canes. Let dry. Clip the rubber bands. Add more hot glue if necessary.

3. Glue smaller candy canes around the top of the holder if desired for a layered effect.

Note: Candy canes should not be eaten after used for crafting. Never leave a burning candle unattended.

PEPPERMINT WISHES GIFT

Who wouldn't love a sweet gift of chocolate-covered peppermint sticks? To make the gift, melt dark chocolate chips in the microwave just until melted (about 1 minute for 1 cup chips). Dip the sticks and sprinkle with crushed peppermint candies or coarse sugar. Lay on parchment paper to dry. Place in a parchment-lined box and add a stamped gift tag clipped on with a red clothespin.

JUMP FOR JOY PILLOW

A playful peppermint-inspired painted design on a fabric square spells out lots of holiday joy.

WHAT YOU NEED

18-inch square of canvas (pillow top) • Newspaper • Acrylic paint: gray, white, yellow, medium green, red, dark green, aqua • Wide paintbrush • Transfer paper: black • Dried-up ballpoint pen or stylus • Artists brushes • Embroidery thread: brown and gold metallic • Sewing machine • Sewing thread: black and red • 19-inch square of white cotton fabric (pillow front) • 75-inch length of pom-pom fringe: red • Two 12×19-inch pieces of red cotton fabric (pillow back) • 18-inch-square pillow form

WHAT YOU DO

TO PAINT THE PILLOW TOP:

1. Lay canvas square on newspaper-covered work surface. Paint the canvas with gray paint, leaving a ½-inch-wide unpainted border around all edges; let dry.
2. Enlarge and trace pattern, right, onto white paper. Lay transfer paper on top of canvas. Lay pattern on top of transfer paper. Using a dried-up ballpoint pen or stylus, trace the letters, tree, and star to transfer the pattern to the canvas. Remove papers.
3. Paint each letter with white paint. Paint the star yellow and the tree medium green. Let dry. Paint red stripes on each letter. Referring to the pattern and using a fine-tip artists brush, paint short dark green wavy lines on the tree. Paint large aqua polka dots randomly on the gray background.

TO EMBELLISH THE PILLOW TOP:

1. Using brown embroidery thread, stitch closely spaced short horizontal straight stitches under the tree for a trunk.
2. Using black sewing thread and a free-motion foot on your sewing machine, stitch an outline around each letter, the star, and the tree.
3. To fray the pillow top edges, pull a few threads from each raw edge.

TO FINISH THE PILLOW:

1. Aligning raw edges and using a ¼-inch seam allowance, sew pom-pom fringe to the right side of the 19-inch white fabric square, overlapping fringe ends.
2. On each 12×19-inch piece of red cotton fabric, hem one 19-inch edge under ¼ inch and then ¼ inch again; press. Place the pillow front faceup. Place red cotton fabric pieces right sides down on top of pillow front, overlapping hemmed edges, sandwiching the pom-pom fringe between the layers, and aligning the raw edges. Using a ½-inch seam allowance and red sewing thread, sew together pillow front and pillow back. Clip the corners and turn pillow cover right side out.
3. Pin the canvas pillow top to the pillow front. Using gold metallic embroidery floss and a running stitch, stitch the pillow top to the pillow front 1 inch from the raw canvas edges. Insert pillow form through the opening in pillow back.

For Stitch Diagrams, see page 160.

This boisterous pillow proudly sings "Joy to the World" for all to hear thanks to its playfully painted design on a fabric square. Pom-pom fringe finishes the vocal pillow with equally merry spirit. The canvas pillow top is painted and embellished, then stitched to the pillow with running stitches.

Jump for Joy Pillow Pattern
Enlarge 200%

Everything Evergreen

Wispy or full, berried or plain, create beautiful and fresh holiday displays by grouping nature's own bits and pieces from the outdoors.

WISPY WELCOME

A sweep of evergreen and herbs combine to make a welcoming wreath with a gentle shape and form.

WHAT YOU NEED
• ¾×12-inch round fiberboard wreath form • Pencil • Coping saw • Fresh and dried greenery and herbs • Floral wire • Hot-glue gun and glue sticks • Twine • Scissors

WHAT YOU DO
1. Lay the wreath form on a flat surface and use a pencil to mark a 10-inch (circumference) area to be removed. Use the saw to cut on the lines. Remove that section.
2. Plan the design by laying the greenery and herbs along the bottom edge of the wreath. Attach with floral wire and, if needed, hot glue. Attach twine to hang.

THREE-SIDED BEAUTY

Floral stems crisscross to form a lovely triangular-shape wreath to adorn your door or hallway.

WHAT YOU NEED
• Paper-wrapped floral stem wire (See Sources, page 160) • Wire snips • Leather cord • Fresh and dried flowers (fresh evergreens, dried eucalyptus, cotton pods) • Floral wire • Hot-glue gun and glue sticks • Ribbon • Scissors

WHAT YOU DO
1. Cut three 9-inch-long sections of floral stem wire. Lay them in a triangle with ends overlapping approximately 1 inch. Tie each intersection together with leather cord.
2. Attach dried and fresh florals with floral wire and, if needed, hot glue. Attach a ribbon to hang.

GREENERY GUIDE

Great wreaths and swags begin with a beautiful assortment of greens. Choose long-needle varieties like white or Scotch pine for background areas and add shorter-needle varieties such as Fraser fir or blue spruce layered on top. Juniper, with its blue berries, and boxwood, with its small leaves, work well with most any wreath or swag.

Juniper

Arborvitae

Blue spruce

Boxwood

White pine

Fraser fir

NATURE INSPIRED

*Peruse the beautiful offerings at your local garden center or farmers market and purchase
a wreath covered with clusters of short-needle greens like balsam. Or for a wreath you can
use for years to come, shop for an everlasting version. Embellish it with as many naturals as
you like, using your hot-glue gun and florists wire. We found it most effective to cluster faux
berries, eucalyptus, Queen Anne's lace blossoms, and dusty miller and then wire each cluster
together, creating about a dozen bunches for the wreath. For a lush and full appearance, tuck
in and glue the bundles along the inner and outer edges as well as on the front.*

SWEET SUCCULENTS

*Wonderfully realistic and easy to find, faux succulents are almost as exciting as the real ones.
To start, purchase a succulent wreath or make your own by hot-gluing artificial plants onto
any evergreen base. With a love of all things vintage, we thought it would be pretty if the plants
looked like they had been "sugared" in the style of Victorian fresh fruit. For this look, brush the
plants with decoupage medium, then sprinkle the wet adhesive with glitter. Once dry, tuck in
snippets of fresh or faux evergreens and both light green and red berry stems.*

SHARE THE JOY

Cookie cutters are wrapped with twine and tied to berries and fresh greenery for a joyful tribute to the holiday season.

WHAT YOU NEED
- 6 star-shape cookie cutters
- Scissors • Narrow twine • Fresh greenery and berries • Floral wire
- "Joy" purchased hanging ornament

WHAT YOU DO
1. Lay the cookie cutters on a flat surface in an arrangement you like. Use the twine to wind around them, tying them in place. Set aside.
2. Lay the greenery and berries in the arrangement you like. Wire the tip with floral wire. Wrap and tie the top with twine, leaving a tail for hanging.
3. Tie the wrapped cookie cutters to the greenery. Tie the "Joy" ornament to the bottom of the cookie cutters.

HERBAL ELEGANCE

Create this wreath, opposite, as a festive addition to any kitchen window. Stack and wire together bundles of rosemary, bay leaves, sage, thyme, oregano, and marjoram and place them, working in a clockwise fashion with all stems pointing in the same direction, around a grapevine wreath form. Finish by tucking in any extra leaves and hanging from ribbon.

Quick Tip: *The fresh herbs used in this wreath will shrink as they dry, so be sure to overstuff each bundle before wiring to the form.*

The beauty of these bundles of greenery is the variety and types of greenery, berries, and herbs that are used. Try using new types of greenery with variegated colors and textures that complement each other.

GARLAND OF GREENS

Little snippets of greenery and berries are bundled together to make a clever holiday garland.

WHAT YOU NEED
• Fresh flowers and/or berries and evergreen • Floral wire • Ribbon • Clothespins • String or yarn • Scissors

WHAT YOU DO
1. Plan the design of the garland by laying the desired greenery, berries, or flowers in bunches.
2. Secure each bundle by wrapping the top of the bunch with floral wire. Tie ribbon into a bow around the bundle to hide the wire.
3. Lay a string or ribbon on a flat surface and clip each bundle onto the string with a clothespin to create the garland.

CASCADING JINGLE BELL SWAG

Create a lovely swag with jingle bells that cascade from top to bottom. Layer various types of evergreens and wire them in place. Then wire together groups of jingle bells and add them to the swag with the large groupings at the top cascading to tiny groupings at the bottom. Tuck in rustic sticks at the top of the swag and wire in place and tie a large bow and wire at the top.

WELCOME WINTER

Remake a simple grapevine wreath into a simple signature of winter with the addition of a few pinecones and a quick coat of silver spray paint. Then nestle evergreen twigs into the wreath. A mix of species such as arborvitae, white pine, juniper, and fir lends instant character. Add a tiny nest and sparkly bird for a finishing touch.

BUILD YOUR NEST

Garden center treasures and crafts supply store finds unite to create these nature-inspired centerpieces. Give a purchased bird nest a quick coat of silver spray paint and fill it with moss and a votive tea light. Snip succulent rosettes from potted plants and tuck them around the nest. The succulents will look fresh for several weeks. Finish with fresh greenery sprigs and silver birds.

WREATH TRIO

Little grapevine wreaths are dressed up with bits of evergreen, sage, rosemary, and thyme. The greenery and herbs can be tucked into the grapevine and wired with green floral wire. Add a twine hanger and let this trio swing in your kitchen window.

MAGICAL FOREST DISPLAY

Sticks from the backyard, acorns, moss ornaments, and twinkles of light combine to make a winter display for your holiday table.

WHAT YOU NEED

Urn or container • Oasis to fit in urn • Sticks • Moss balls (available at crafts stores) • Straight pins • Brown string • Moss sheets (available at crafts stores) • White Christmas lights • Linen fabric • Acorns

WHAT YOU DO

1. Place the Oasis in the urn and cut to fit. Place the sticks into the Oasis at desired height.

2. Lay the moss balls on a flat surface and use straight pins to attach string for hanging. Hang the balls on the sticks.

3. Cover the surface of the Oasis with the sheet moss. Cut to fit.

4. Surround the urn with white lights. Lay the linen fabric over the lights. Add acorns and sticks to the arrangement.

PRETTY IN PINK

A fresh evergreen wreath is dressed up for the season with painted pinecones, velvet ribbon, and clusters of mini ornaments.

WHAT YOU NEED

Fresh evergreen wreath • Small pinecones • Pink crafts paint • Paintbrush • Floral wire • Small ornaments in pink, gold and silver • Narrow pink velvet ribbon • Fresh or artificial succulent plants • Wide ribbon for bow

WHAT YOU DO

1. Lay the evergreen wreath on a flat surface and plan the design. Paint desired number of small pinecones and let dry. Set aside.

2. Use floral wire to group small ornaments. Set aside.

3. Wrap wreath with velvet ribbon, securing in back. Wire pinecones. Attach pinecones and groups of small ornaments. Tuck in and wire succulent plants.

4. Tie a bow and attach at the top. Add a ribbon for hanging.

RETRO ACTIVE

Back in the '50s, tin reflectors gave tree lights extra twinkle and color to showcase the tree. These little reflectors can become mini ball ornaments to dress up a plain evergreen wreath. Place a mini ornament in the center hole of a reflector and attach it to the wreath with florists wire. Wire assorted sizes and colors of ornaments to the wreath for extra color and dimension. You can find vintage reflectors online or reproductions of these shiny showstoppers in crafts stores.

GNOME WELCOME

Little gnomes sit as elves waiting to greet all that come to call. To make the wreath see below. To make the gnomes, see page 139.

WHAT YOU NEED

Fresh evergreen wreath • Jingle bells • Red glitter • Crafts glue • Acorn tops • Frosted artificial berries on stem • Florists wire • Wide burlap ribbon • Wide red ribbon • Gnomes (see page 139 for instructions)

WHAT YOU DO

1. Lay the wreath on a flat surface to plan the design. Spread glue on desired number of jingle bells and dust with glitter. Let dry. Glue to the inside of the acorn tops. Let dry. Wire the acorns. Set aside.
2. Wire the berries on the stem at the bottom of the wreath. Wire in the acorn tops.
3. Set the gnomes at the bottom of the wreath. Wire in place.
4. Lay the two ribbons together and tie in a large bow. Wire at the top of the wreath.

SIMPLE ELEGANCE

Rosemary puts a fresh and fragrant spin on a classic laurel-style wreath that will become a front door's crowning glory. Hot glue the inner and outer rings of a 14-inch wooden quilting hoop together; let dry. Cut an 8-inch section out of the top of the glued-together hoop. Use florists wire to attach rosemary bunches to the sides of the hoop and sprigs to the front. Glue a bow to the bottom center of the wreath.

Common galvanized chicken wire wraps into a cone to become the structure for a rustic woodland tree shape for a farmhouse-style accent piece. Fresh cedar sprigs tuck into the wire while little lights surround the handsome piece.

WOODLAND WHIMSY

A chicken-wire cone peeks out from the wispy greenery as it falls from this evergreen display topped with a pinecone star.

WHAT YOU NEED

Galvanized chicken wire (available at home stores) • Wire cutters • Burlap or bark-style ribbon • Battery lights • Fresh evergreen pieces • Wire • Small pinecones • Hot-glue gun and glue sticks • Anise star

WHAT YOU DO

1. Cut an 18×18-inch piece of chicken wire. Wrap it into a cone shape. Secure with wire. Trim edges.
2. Wind a burlap or bark-style ribbon around the chicken-wire cone. Secure with wire or glue. Wind the lights around the wire.
3. Tuck pieces of greenery and pinecones into the chicken wire and secure with wire.
4. To make the pinecone star, lay the pinecones into a star shape and secure with glue. Glue the anise star in the middle.

Merry and Bright

A bold color palette and happy winter motifs shed new light on brilliant ways to celebrate the season.

THE SHAPES OF WINTER

Light wood candlesticks with bright-colored candles and bottle-brush trees march across a mantel in a vibrant winter scene.

WHAT YOU NEED

2×3-inch wooden cones (See Sources, page 160, for all wood items) • 1½×⅛-inch wooden washers • ¾-inch wooden beehive beads • 1¹⁄₁₆-inch wooden finials or dowel cap ends • 1¾-inch wooden British knobs • Small (2¼-inch) wooden bean pots • Wooden doll pin stands • Quick-setting or wood glue • Assorted candles • Assorted bottle-brush trees • Crafts glue

WHAT YOU DO

1. Referring to the photo, above, layer wooden pieces to form candleholders of different heights. Place the bottle-brush trees or candles temporarily in the holders to see how they look. When satisfied with the arrangements, glue together wood pieces with quick-setting or wood glue; let dry for several hours.

2. Glue candles and bottle-brush trees into tops of candleholders using crafts glue.

JOYFUL BOTTLE-BRUSH WRAP

WHAT YOU NEED

Colored bottle brush-trees • Crafts paint in desired colors (optional) • Gift wrap in an assortment of colors • Hot-glue gun and glue sticks • Ribbon • Scissors

WHAT YOU DO

1. If the bottle brush tree comes with a wood bottom, paint the bottom of the tree in desired color. Let dry.

2. Wrap the gift in a coordinating color of gift wrap. Use scissors to trim the back of the tree until you have a flat surface. Attach tree to gift wrap using hot glue.

3. Wrap ribbon around the package to finish.

MARBLEIZED PAPER CONES

WHAT YOU NEED

Disposable pan large enough to accommodate cardstock
• Nail polish (2 or 3 colors) • Toothpicks • White cardstock
• Paper towels • Iron • Hot-glue gun and glue sticks •
Rickrack in color to coordinate with papers • Scissors
• Crafts glue • Candy canes

WHAT YOU DO

1. Fill disposable pan halfway full of water. Drop several drops
of nail polish into the water. Working quickly, create swirls in
the nail polish using a toothpick. Gently place cardstock on
top of water, pressing out any air bubbles. Gently lift the paper
out of the water. Lay on paper towels. Let dry.

2. When dry, place one dry paper towel on top of and one
below the paper. Using a cool iron, press out any wrinkles.
Cool completely.

3. Enlarge and trace desired size template, below, and cut out.
Trace onto marbled paper and cut out. Attach sides together
using hot glue to form the cone.

3. Cut a piece of rickrack to fit around the top of the cone. Glue
on the inside of the cone. Use crafts glue to adhere a candy
cane to the inside of the cone for a handle.

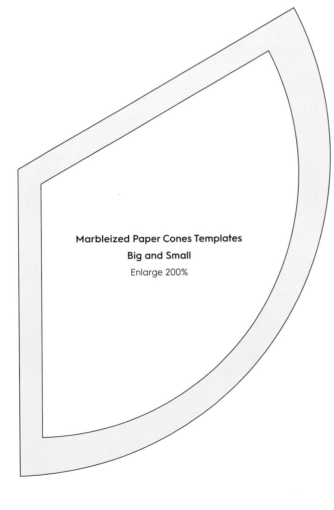

Marbleized Paper Cones Templates
Big and Small
Enlarge 200%

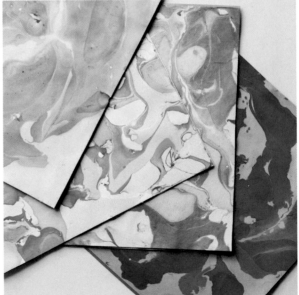

HOW TO MAKE A TASSEL

1. Wrap yarn many times around cardboard or a book. Tie into a bundle at one end; cut other end (A).
2. Wrap yarn around the bundle several times near the tied end; tie in place (B).
3. Trim the loose ends of the yarn to the desired tassel length (C).

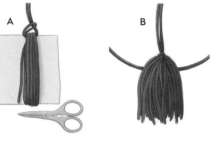

WINTER RING TONES

Two sizes of ball knobs and an embroidery hoop become a focal point with little time and effort. Bead-embellished tassels and pom-poms complete the wreath in up-to-date colors.

WHAT YOU NEED

Two 12-inch wooden embroidery hoops • Thirty-nine 1-inch-diameter wooden ball knobs • Nineteen 1¼-inch-diameter wooden ball knobs • Hot-glue gun and glue sticks • Yarn in coral, gold, red, and light blue • 5-inch cardboard square • Four assorted ⅛-inch to ¼-inch round wooden beads

WHAT YOU DO

MAKE THE WREATH

1. Remove and discard the screw and inner ring from one embroidery hoop (or reserve for another use).
2. Aligning hardware, place outer ring around outside of intact embroidery hoop to make a wreath form.
3. With embroidery hoop hardware at top of wreath form, hot-glue a 1¼-inch (large) wooden knob to bottom center of form. Referring to photo, above, dab hot glue to the left of the large knob and immediately add two 1-inch (small) knobs;

hold beads in place until glue sets. Dab hot glue to the right of the large knob and add two more small knobs. Continue alternating one large knob and two small knobs and work up both sides of the wreath. At the top, fill any open space with a small knob.

MAKE THE TASSELS, POM-POM, AND HANGER

1. Referring to "How to Make a Tassel," above, and "Three-Tier Tassel," page 79, with coral, gold, and red yarn (without dyed beads) make tassels. Tie twine tail to top of wreath so tassel hangs in the wreath center.
2. Referring to "How to Make a Pom-Pom," opposite, use gold yarn to make a pom-pom. Thread three round beads onto both tails and tie pom-pom to top of wreath.
3. Referring to "How to Make a Tassel," above, make a single tassel by wrapping several colors of yarn around the 5-inch cardboard square. Thread a 10-inch length of yarn under the wraps along one cardboard edge; tie tightly into a knot, leaving long tails. Cut through wraps at opposite edge of square. Wrap red yarn around tassel near the tied end; tie in place. Thread remaining round wooden bead onto tassel tails; tie tassel to top of wreath.
4. For a hanger, tie a doubled length of yarn in desired color and wrap around top of wreath.

HEARTH STRINGS

Dress a holiday mantel with graceful lengths of beads, tiered tassels, and pom-poms.

HOW TO MAKE A POM-POM

1. Wrap yarn many times around a fork, book, or other object depending on the size of pom-pom desired (A).
2. Tie the entire bundle in the center and slide the yarn from the object (B).
3. Cut the looped yarn at both ends of the bundle (C).
4. Trim yarn ends to desired length (D). Fluff the yarn.

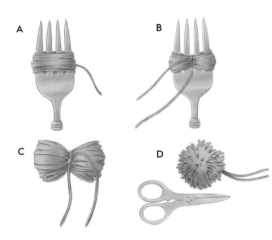

THREE-TIER TASSEL

WHAT YOU NEED
• Liquid dye (such as RIT): cherry red and aquamarine • Disposable container • Two ½×¾-inch oval wooden beads • 5-inch cardboard square • Yarn: red, gold, coral • Yarn needle • Cotton or hemp twine • Two ¼-inch round wooden beads • ½-inch round wooden bead • ¾-inch wooden beehive bead

WHAT YOU DO

MAKE THE TASSEL
1. Referring to "Dye the Beads," below, dye one oval bead cherry red and one oval bead aquamarine.
2. Wrap one color of yarn around cardboard square 20 to 30 times. Thread a 10-inch length of yarn under the wraps along one cardboard edge; tie tightly into a knot. Cut through wraps at opposite edge of square. Leave tassel 5 inches long. Repeat to make two more tassels, each in a different color. Trim second tassel to 4 inches long; trim third tassel to 3 inches long.
3. Thread the yarn needle with a 12-inch length of twine; knot the end. Push the needle up through the center of the 5-inch-long tassel; push tassel to knot. Thread on the 4-inch tassel and then the 3-inch tassel so tassels overlap.

DYE THE BEADS
1. In a disposable container stir together 2 to 3 capfuls of aquamarine liquid dye and 1 to 2 cups of boiling water. String four oval wooden beads onto a piece of florists wire and curve the wire into a circle. Holding the top of the circle, dip the beads into the dye; agitate beads gently in dye for 1 to 2 minutes. Set beads on a paper towel; let dry. **Note:** Color will lighten during drying process.
2. Repeat with apple green liquid dye and remaining oval beads.

MAKE A POM-POM
Referring to "How to Make a Pom-Pom," left, wrap gold yarn around the tines of a fork at least 10 times. Thread an 8-inch length of gold yarn between the tines and tie it around the wraps. Cut through the wraps along both edges of fork; remove pom-pom from fork. Trim pom-pom, leaving the two long tails. Thread one ¼-inch, one ½-inch, and another ¼-inch bead onto both tails.

ADD MORE BEADS
Cut three 6-inch lengths of twine. Tie the lengths together in a knot at one end and thread the red oval bead onto the twine; push to the knot. Hold together the tails on the three-tiered tassel, the pom-pom, and the red oval bead; adjust the length of each piece and tie tails together in a knot about 1½ inches above the oval bead. Thread the tails through the beehive bead and blue oval bead. Tie another knot above the beads.

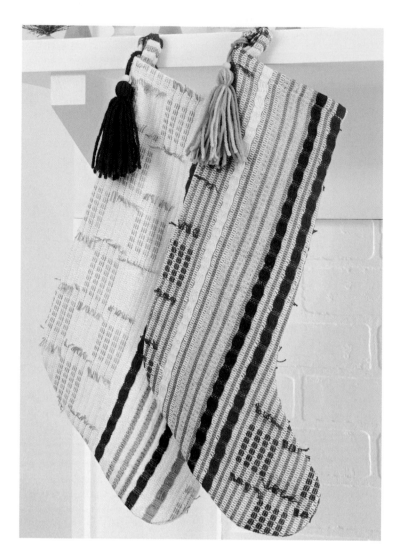

STOCKING SURPRISE

WHAT YOU NEED (FOR ONE STOCKING)
• White paper • Scissors • Two cotton tea towels
• Matching sewing thread • Yarn in red, green, and/
or gold • 5-inch cardboard square • 1¼-inch round
wooden bead

WHAT YOU DO
1. Enlarge the stocking pattern, right, onto white
paper; cut out. Layer tea towels with right sides
together and trace pattern onto tea towels, using
a hemmed edge as the stocking top.
2. With right sides together, sew around edges,
leaving top open; turn right side out.
3. To make a hanging loop, cut a 2×7-inch strip from
leftover tea towel. Fold both long edges to center and then
fold lengthwise in half to enclose raw edges; topstitch. Fold in
half crosswise and stitch short raw edges inside stocking top.
4. Tie on a bead-accented yarn tassel (see "How to Make a
Tassel," page 78).

**Stocking Surprise
Pattern**

Enlarge 300%
Cut 2

MATCH GAME PACKAGES

Use your tassel- and pom-pom-making talents to make toppers for bright and cheery Christmas packages. With so many colors of yarn, it is easy to make perfectly coordinated toppers for your packages. Follow the instructions for making tassels and pom-poms on pages 78 and 79.

REINDEER-PLAY JARS

Tiny plastic reindeer figurines are painted happy colors and glued to jars for creative gift containers.

WHAT YOU NEED
Miniature reindeers (available at crafts stores) • Jars with lids
• Spray paint • Hot-glue gun and glue sticks

WHAT YOU DO
1. Lay reindeers and jar lids on a covered surface and spray with paint. Let dry.
2. Position the painted reindeer on top of the lid and attach using hot glue. Let dry.

EAGER ELVES

These rosy-cheeked fellows work up quickly using felt and embroidery floss with jingling bells atop their elfin hats, of course.

WHAT YOU NEED (FOR ONE ELF)

4×9-inch pieces of felt: light pink (head), red and green (hat and hatband), yellow or tan (hair) • Fabric glue • Embroidery floss: light pink, red, and green • Embroidery needle • 2 black 6-millimeter shank-back safety doll eyes • Acrylic paint: red • Round artists brush • Straight pins • ⅜-inch-diameter gold bell • Polyester fiberfill

WHAT YOU DO

1. Enlarge and trace patterns, right, onto white paper; cut out. Trace each shape on appropriate felt color the number of times indicated on pattern. Cut out the shapes on traced lines.

2. Lay pieces, excluding hair, out in two matching sets. Flip the pieces of one set over so you have one set for the front and one set for the back.

3. Referring to the photo, right, and dashed placement lines on the pattern, glue a hat to each head. Glue hair below the hat on head front. Glue the hatband over hat/hair edge on head front and over bottom of hat on head back.

4. On wrong side of each head piece, trim away about ⅛ inch of light pink felt along hat and hatband edges. Use matching embroidery floss to whipstitch along long hatband edges on right side of each head piece.

5. Using one strand of red embroidery floss, stem-stitch a mouth on the head front. Carefully poke a tiny hole for each eye. Insert an eye shank through each hole. Slide the washer onto the shank. Trim each shank, leaving about ⅛ inch.

6. Dip a dry round brush into red paint, then blot brush on a paper towel until little paint shows. Dry-brush color onto cheeks.

7. Pin the head front to head back with wrong sides together. Starting at top of hatband on one side of head, use one strand of matching embroidery floss to whipstitch pieces together. Work down around elf face, switching embroidery floss colors as needed. When you reach the hat tip, add a jingle bell as you stitch, securing it with extra stitches before continuing to whipstitch. Leave a 1½-inch opening along the last side of hat. Using the eraser end of a pencil, push fiberfill through the opening until elf is lightly stuffed. Whipstitch opening closed.

8. Cut a 9-inch length of embroidery floss for a hanging loop. Stitch the floss through the hat tip and knot the ends.

For Stitch Diagrams, see page 160.

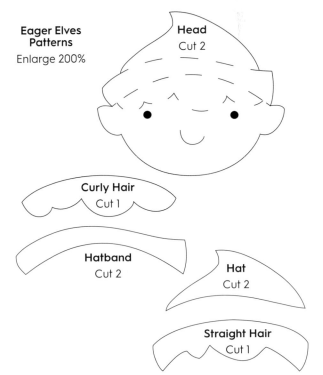

Eager Elves Patterns

Enlarge 200%

Head
Cut 2

Curly Hair
Cut 1

Hatband
Cut 2

Hat
Cut 2

Straight Hair
Cut 1

LITTLE GREEN GUMDROP WREATH

Just big enough to sit on your counter, this soft and sweet wreath is a cinch to make.

WHAT YOU NEED

Felted wool balls (see Sources, page 160) • Sharp scissors • 8-inch flat wreath form • Angora yarn in shades of green • Crafts glue or fabric glue

WHAT YOU DO

1. Using sharp scissors, cut the wool balls in half. Set aside.
2. Lay the wreath form on a flat surface. Tape one end of the yarn to the wreath. Begin wrapping the wreath all the way around until the entire wreath is covered. Secure with glue.
3. Plan the design on the wreath and then glue the balls, flat sides down, onto the wreath. Let dry.

SOFT-AND-SWEET GUMDROP PILLOW

A cast-off angora sweater finds a happy new life dressed up with bright felted wool balls.

WHAT YOU NEED

Cast-off wool sweater, wool fabric, or purchased wool pillow • 12×12-inch pillow form • Thread to match fabric • Felted wool balls (see Sources, page 160) • Sharp scissors • Crafts glue or fabric glue

WHAT YOU DO

1. Using sharp scissors, cut the wool balls in half. Set aside.
2. To make the pillow, cut two 14×14-inch pieces of fabric from the sweater or fabric. With right sides together, stitch around the pillow, leaving an opening for turning. Turn pillow; press. Slide pillow form inside pillow. Sew opening closed.
3. Plan the design on the pillow and glue the balls, flat sides down, onto the pillow. Let dry.

JOYFUL ORNAMENT DISPLAY

Colorful Christmas ornaments in all sizes and styles are perched in mismatched wineglasses for a sparkling display. Use vintage or new ornaments and showcase the display as a centerpiece or on a mantel.

BRIGHT BRANCHES GIFT WRAP

A winter walk in the woods to find some sticks will be the inspiration for these clever wraps. Paint the sticks with crafts paint and let dry. Then glue mini pom-poms to the sticks. Choose brightly colored gift wrap and then tie on the sticks with colorful twine.

RETRO CHIC HOLIDAY TRIMS

These trims may be old school but not old-fashioned. These bright holiday gems combine classic techniques with forward-thinking color schemes and designs.

WHAT YOU NEED

• Sport-weight 100% cotton yarn: assorted colors • Size C/2 (2.75-millimeter) crochet hook • 3-inch round ornament with ornament cap and hanging loop • Yarn needle

Note: See Crochet Abbreviations, below.
Spike stitch: Insert hook between 2 dc from rnd 2, yo, draw up a lp to the same height as the working row, and draw through both lps on hook.

WHAT YOU DO

MAKE A HALF BALL
Note: Make two half balls. Each half ball will start to curve slightly after rnd 5. Fit half ball to ornament to check sizing; it should have some ease to stretch. Adding or removing sc rows can help with fit.

USING FIRST COLOR, MAKE A MAGIC RING.
Rnd 1: Ch 3 (counts as 1 dc), make 11 dc in magic ring, sl st to top of beg ch 3 to join. Pull magic ring tightly to close. Fasten off (12 dc).
Rnd 2: Using new color, join in any st from rnd 1. Ch 3 (counts as 1 dc), 1 dc in same st, 2 dc in each st around, sl st to top of beg ch 3 to join. Fasten off (24 dc).
Rnd 3: Using new color, join in sp between any of the sets of 2 dc from rnd 2. Ch 3 (counts as 1 dc), 1 dc in same sp, ch 1, miss next 2 sts *2 dc in next sp, ch 1, miss 2 sts; rep from * around, sl st to top of beg ch 3 to join. Fasten off yarn. (24 dc, 12 ch 1)
Rnd 4: Using new color, join in top of first dc from any 2 dc set in rnd 3, ch 1, 1 sc in same st, 1 sc in next st, 1 spike stitch in ch 1 sp, inserting hook between 2 dc from rnd 2, *1 sc in next 2 sts, 1 spike stitch, repeat from * 10 more times, sl st to first sc to join. Fasten off (24 sc, 12 spike st).
Rnds 5–7: Using new color, join in any st. Ch 1, 1 sc in each st around. Sl st to first sc to join. Fasten off (36 sc).
Weave in all ends.

FINISHING
With right sides facing out, slip both crocheted half balls onto the round ornament. Using a matching yarn color and a yarn needle, stitch the half balls together, leaving a space for the ornament cap and hanging loop. Fasten off and weave in ends.

CROCHET ABBREVIATIONS

BEG	begin(ning)	**REP**	repeat
CH	chain	**RND(S)**	round(s)
CONT	continue	**SC**	single crochet
DC	double crochet	**SL ST**	slip stitch
HDC	half double crochet	**SP**	space
INC	increase	**ST(S)**	stitch(es)
LP(S)	loop(s)	**YO**	yarn over

The Complete Package

Reach out to the ones you love with handmade cards, gifts, and personalized wraps they will treasure forever.

PERFECTLY PLAID
GREETING CARDS

WHAT YOU NEED

White cardstock • Pencil • Scissors • Plaid-patterned scrapbooking paper • Double-sided tape • Stamp and ink pad or gold marker

WHAT YOU DO

1. Trace or copy the tree card templates, right. Trace onto patterned cardstock and cut out.

2. Fold white cardstock and position the trees onto the card where desired. Attach using double-sided tape, overlapping trees on the white cardstock.

3. Stamp or print a message on the front of the card if desired.

Note: Card can also be framed to display or give as a gift.

**Perfectly Plaid
Greeting Cards
Patterns**

RICKRACK COASTERS
Scraps of favorite quilt fabrics become useful coasters all trimmed out with coordinating rickrack.

WHAT YOU NEED (FOR ONE COASTER)
4×4-inch piece of fusable cotton batting ● Two 5×5-inch pieces of small print cotton fabric ● Iron ● 24-inch piece of rickrack in coordinating color ● Sewing machine

WHAT YOU DO
1. Fuse the piece of cotton batting to the wrong side of one of the pieces of print fabric. Layer the two pieces with wrong sides together. Turn under ⅜ inch on all sides of the fabric pieces. Press.
2. Place the rickrack between the pressed edges. Topstitch around the layered pieces, catching the rickrack in the stitching. Press.

PUPPY TOYS

Make some special toys for your furry best friend to play with all Christmas day.

WHAT YOU NEED

FOR THE BRAIDED TOY
Three 18-inch pieces of wool felt or heavy flannel in desired colors • Tape • Leather or felt for tying

FOR THE BALL TOY
12×12-inch piece of heavy flannel • Tennis ball • Rubber band • Scissors • Piece of leather or felt for tying

WHAT YOU DO

FOR THE BRAIDED TOY
1. Tape the three ends of the felt or flannel together at the top. Braid the strips together.
2. Remove the tape and tie the ends with leather cording or strips of felt.

FOR THE BALL TOY
1. Lay the piece of flannel on a table with the ball in the center. Bring the corners of the square around the ball and secure with a rubber band to temporarily hold in place.
2. Tie tightly with a strip of leather or flannel. Cut off the rubber band and throw it away.

PAW PRINT WRAP

Choose a brown paper sack and an ink stamp pad. Press your thumb twice to make the center of the paw print and your fingers to make the four other prints. Write the puppy's name on the sack. Fill with toys and doggie treats.

REVERSIBLE SNUGGLE SCARF

Show off your sewing and crochet skills by stitching this cozy scarf using two different patterns of fabric and a sweet crochet edging.

WHAT YOU NEED

½ to 1½ yards of flannel in two patterns of fabric*
• Sewing machine • Yarn to coordinate with fabrics
• Crochet needle (size I)

*Flannel can vary from ½ to 1½ yards based on using 45-inch-wide fabric. The scarf shown is 54×9 inches, which would require 1½ yards of each patterned fabric. **Note:** If you want to make the scarf shorter (42×9 inches), you would only need ¼ yard of each patterned fabric. The average length for a scarf is between 40 and 60 inches long.

WHAT YOU DO

1. Cut two pieces of fabric, each 54×9-inches (for longer scarf) or 42×9-inch pieces (for shorter scarf). With right sides together and using ½-inch seam, sew around perimeter, allowing a small opening at the end. Turn inside out and hand-stitch closed. Press. Topstitch around the perimeter of scarf using a ½-inch seam.

2. Use yarn to work the blanket stitch to embroider around both ends of the scarf, knotting at the beginning and at the end of the row.

3. To crochet the ends, with yarn, make a slip knot on crochet hook. Insert hook into the center of the first blanket stitch. Work your way down the row, using a half double crochet stitch. At the end of the row, turn the scarf over and make one chain stitch. Work your way down the row, using a double crochet stitch. At the end of the row, turn the scarf over and make four chain stitches. Slip stitch into the next stitch. As you work your way down the row, chain four and slip stitch into every other stitch. At the end of the row, cut the yarn, leaving 6-inch tail at the end. Draw the hook straight up, bringing the yarn through the remaining loop on the hook. Weave the extra yarn into the stitches, trimming when complete.

SCARF GIFT WRAP

Wrap the lid and the bottom of the box in a paper that coordinates with the scarf. Crisscross the ribbon and tape on the inside of the box. Form a loop with the ribbon and use double-stick tape to secure.

PRANCING REINDEER PILLOW

Reindeer motifs are stamped onto a fabric pillow case trimmed with red rickrack to make a perfect gift for any Rudolf lover.

WHAT YOU NEED

Craft foam • Block of wood or small sturdy box • Spray adhesive • Scissors • Brown crafts paint • Foam paint brush • Mini red pom-poms • Hot-glue gun and glue sticks • ½ yard cream fabric or heavy muslin • Parchment paper • Thread to match fabric • Red jumbo rickrack • Scissors • Pillow insert

WHAT YOU DO

1. To make the stamp, trace the template, right, and cut out. Cut the reindeer shape out of crafts foam and mount to block of wood using spray adhesive. **Tip:** To make the stamp thicker, use multiple layers—cut three reindeer shapes from crafts foam and glue to each other before adhering to the wood or box. Set aside.

2. To make the pillow, cut two 16×16-inch pieces of fabric. Lay one piece of the fabric on a parchment-lined table. Paint crafts paint onto stamp using a foam brush (paint liberally) or dip into paint and stamp onto fabric. Let dry. When dry, attach red pom-poms to nose using hot-glue gun.

3. Lay the rickrack on the back pillow piece with the stitching line ½ inch in from the edge. Baste in place on stitching line. With right sides together, place the printed pillow on top of the back piece. Stitch around the edge of the pillow on the stitching line, leaving one side open for turning. Turn. Slide pillow insert into the pillow case. Whip-stitch opening closed.

Prancing Reindeer Pillow Template

FRESH-SCENT POTPOURRI BAGS

*Whether you like the sweet scent of cinnamon and anise
or the savory aroma of caraway and rosemary, these bags
of fresh scents are fun to make and will please everyone
on your gift-giving list.*

WHAT YOU NEED
Cinnamon sticks • Whole cloves • Anise stars • Coffee beans
• Dried oranges • Caraway seeds • Bay leaves • Dried
rosemary • Cellophane bag • Small scoop • Twine

WHAT YOU DO
1. In a small bowl combine either sweet or savory items. Pour
the mixture into the cellophane bag.
2. Tie cinnamon sticks or a small scoop on the bag with twine
and add a gift tag.

SPLASHY NOTE CARD SET

These easy-to-make note cards can be created by the dozens and sent to favorite friends or tied up with ribbon and given as gift sets.

WHAT YOU NEED

Food coloring in desired colors • Water and bowl • Foam paintbrush • Note card and envelope set • Pen or marker • Narrow metallic ribbon • Scissors

WHAT YOU DO

1. Mix food coloring and water (start with a few drops and add more until desired color is achieved).
2. Dip foam paintbrush into coloring mixture. Lightly dab onto note cards and envelopes in desired pattern. Let dry. Hand-letter a holiday saying onto the card. Tie sets together with ribbon if giving as a gift.

WOOD-BURNED KITCHEN SET

Purchased cutting boards and spoons become works of art when they are embellished with simple designs using a wood-burning tool.

WHAT YOU NEED

Practice paper • Pencil • Practice piece of wood • Purchased wood items such as cutting board, spoons, and other utensils • Wood-burning tool (available at crafts stores and online)

WHAT YOU DO

1. Plan the design of the pieces by sketching designs on a piece of paper or refer to our sketches, opposite. Choose designs that are simple and require only one stroke of the tool tip at a time.
2. Practice the designs on a scrap piece of wood before starting. Try various tool tips if desired.
3. Very lightly, using a pencil, draw the area to be wood-burned. Then following the manufacturer's instructions use the wood-burning tool to create the designs.
Note: Wood-burning tools get very hot. Be sure that all work areas are covered and the stand tool is always used. Never change tool tips until the tool is completely cooled. The tips stay hot for a long time after the tool is shut off.

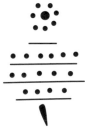

Pattern
Ideas

TIE-ON TASSEL

WHAT YOU NEED

Unfinished wooden ring • Variegated embroidery floss • Colored bead • Quick-setting glue • Holiday card remnant • Mini wooden stars • Faux greenery

WHAT YOU NEED

1. Overlap two widths of ribbon. Secure with tape to the underside of a wrapped package.

2. For the tassel ornament, cut and reserve a length of floss long enough to wrap around the package plus an additional 12 to 14 inches for assembling the tassel. Do not unfold the remaining floss. From the 14-inch length, cut a 4- to 5-inch piece and run it through one end fold of the remaining floss skein. Tie it in a knot and then tie it to the bottom of the wooden ring.

3. Cut another small length of floss and wrap it snugly around the tassel six times about ¼ to ½ inch from the fold. Trim to the desired length.

4. Cut 7 to 8 inches of floss. Tie it in a knot around the top of the ring, slide a bead over the floss, and knot the ends into a bow.

5. Print and cut out a message or use the image or message from one of last year's cards for the ring center. Glue it in place on the underside. Glue mini stars in place. Let the glue dry.

6. Wrap floss around the package and tie it in a bow. Glue the bow knot to the ribbon to keep it in place. Tuck greenery under the bow. Glue if desired.

EMBROIDERY FLOSS TREE

WHAT YOU NEED
14-count perforated cross-stitch paper • Green embroidery floss • Embroidery needle • Tree template • Hot-glue gun and glue sticks

WHAT YOU DO
1. Copy the template, right. Place on perforated paper and cut around it. Thread the needle with floss and stitch along the perimeter as shown in photo. Finish by stitching in the center using a simple outline stitch.
Note: When working on perforated paper, some stitchers prefer to trace on the design, stitch, and then cut out the shape.
2. Knot the floss on the back and trim. Tie your wrapped package with narrow ribbon or cording. Hot-glue the tree to the ribbon.

**Embroidery Floss
Tree Template**

Enlarge 200%

VISIONS OF SUGAR

A yummy bubble gum candy cane makes the perfect topper for pink, red, and white gift wrap. Finish with red ribbon and a sprig of greenery and berries.

WHITE CHRISTMAS

Reminiscent of a vintage feather tree, sprigs of pine are pretty when sprayed with matte-finish white paint. Once dry, add a red berry bunch and sheer ribbon— sheer beauty!

BIRDS OF A FEATHER

All-occasion gift paper can be as beautiful at Christmastime as any other. Cutting out a graphic from the wrap provides a coordinating element for a tag, and red berries make it holiday ready.

JOSEPHINE KNOT

WHAT YOU NEED
Narrow cording in two colors • Double-stick tape

WHAT YOU DO
1. From a decorative paper, cut an accent piece slightly smaller than the wrapped package top. Attach it with double-stick tape.
2. Cut four lengths of cord in the first color and two in the second color. Cut them long enough to go around the package, plus extra for your knot work. Divide the cording into two sets of three strands each. You will treat each set as one piece. Make a loop with the first piece. Place the loop over the second piece. Weave the second piece over the lower loop tail, under the upper loop tail, over the upper loop, under the beginning of the second piece, and over the lower loop.
3. Position the knot on the package. Pull the loose ends to the back of the package and tape. To finish, bring a single piece of cord from back to front and run the ends through the middle of the knot. Tie the ends to secure.

Corrugated Bow Template

Enlarge 300%

CHENILLE POINSETTIA

WHAT YOU NEED

4 red chenille bump stems • Thin wire • 7 wooden 8 mm beads • Hot-glue gun and glue sticks

WHAT YOU DO

1. Fold each end of a stem to the center; twist the ends around the center. (This creates two petals.) Repeat with three more chenille stems to make eight petals.

2. Layer the double petal pieces in pairs to form an X. Wire the pairs together at the center. Attach one bead to the center with wire. String six more beads onto a length of wire and attach to the center.

3. Shape the petals as desired (we pinched the petal tips) and glue the flower to the package ribbon.

CORRUGATED BOW

WHAT YOU NEED

Corrugated paper • Bow template

WHAT YOU DO

1. Cut two strips of double-sided corrugated paper to fit your box. Hot-glue the ends to the box bottom. Print and cut out the bow template, trace it onto corrugated paper, and cut out.

2. Fold and glue the ends to the center to create the bow. Wrap a third strip tightly around the center of the bow and glue to the "ribbon" strip on the box.

CLEVER ACORN WRAP

*Acorn tops become holders for unexpected round shapes
to decorate Christmas gift wraps with flair.*

WHAT YOU NEED

Acorn tops • Jingle bells, large beads, wool balls, etc., to fit
into the acorn tops • Crafts glue • Ribbon • Hot-glue gun
and glue sticks

WHAT YOU DO

1. Wrap the package as desired. Wrap the ribbon around the
package, leaving a flat area in the middle.
2. Be sure the insides of the acorn tops are clean and dry. Use
crafts glue to glue the bells or beads inside the tops to create
the embellishment. Let dry.
3. Hot-glue the acorn embellishment where the ribbon crosses
on the package.

Christmas of White

Pure as the driven snow, crafts and decor in all shades of white sparkle with the season.

P·E·A·C·E

ALL-IN-WHITE PAPER TREES

Little squares of paper in all shades of white stack together to make a light and wintry tree.

WHAT YOU NEED

Paper in different shades of white such as scrapbook paper and vellum • Scissors • Foam block such as Styrofoam • Bamboo skewer • Small round piece of birch wood • Drill and small drill bit • Crafts glue

WHAT YOU DO

1. For the taller tree, cut small squares of paper that begin with 4 inches and decrease by ⅛ inch, cutting three squares of each size. Cut about 60 squares for the tall tree. For the shorter tree, cut squares starting at 3½ inches and decrease by ⅛ inch, cutting three squares of each size. Cut about 50 squares.

2. Cut a small star shape for the top.

3. Place the bamboo skewer into the foam block and thread the papers onto the skewer starting at the bottom with the largest squares and ending with the small squares. Add the star at the top. Remove from the foam base. Add a drop of crafts glue at each end of the skewer to secure.

4. Drill a small hole in the round piece of wood. Place a dot of glue in the hole and push the skewer into the hole.

WINTER COZY WREATH

Soft yarn in shades of white wraps snuggly around a wreath form to make a wintery decoration for a shelf or door.

WHAT YOU NEED
Round foam wreath form such as Styrofoam • Soft yarn in shades of white and cream (See Sources, page 160) • Scissors • Straight pins

WHAT YOU DO
1. Decide on the shades of white yarn to be used. Unwind the skeins of yarn and, grouping three strands at once, pin to the top of the form. Wrapping all three strands at a time, wrap around the entire form and pin a the end.
2. Fill in areas with single strands of yarn, pinning in place. Tie a bow at the top of the wreath.

MAKE AN IMPRESSION

Polymer clay is the medium used to make these stunning ornaments with herb impressions as the design element. The trims are rolled out like cookie dough—so fun and easy to make.

WHAT YOU NEED
Parchment paper • Ivory-color polymer clay • Rolling pin • Herbs • Round cookie cutter • Drinking straw • Baking sheet • Acrylic paint: gold metallic • Paper plate • Ribbon

WHAT YOU DO
1. Break off a piece of polymer clay and place on parchment paper. Using a rolling pin, roll clay until it's about ⅛ inch thick. Position herb sprigs on top of the clay, filling the space without too much overlapping. Gently roll over the herbs with a rolling pin, then peel herbs from clay.
2. Use a cookie cutter to cut out round shape, positioning impression inside the circle where desired. Push the end of a drinking straw through the top of the circle to cut a hole for hanging. Place circle on a baking sheet. Repeat to make the desired number of ornaments.
3. Referring to the clay manufacturer's instructions, bake the clay, then let cool completely.
4. Squeeze a thin line of gold metallic paint onto a paper plate. Roll the edge of each ornament in the paint; let dry.
5. Tie a ribbon through the hole in each ornament for a hanging loop.

PLAYFUL STARFISH WREATH

Natural starfish become the stars of the season when they are painted, glittered, and layered to become a shimmering holiday wreath.

WHAT YOU NEED

Natural starfish (available at crafts stores) • Cream-color chalk paint • Paintbrush • Crafts glue • White glitter • Flat fiberboard wreath form • Hot-glue gun and glue sticks • Ribbon for hanging

WHAT YOU DO

1. Lay the starfish on a covered surface and paint both sides. Let dry.

2. Mix 3 tablespoons paint, 1 tablespoon crafts glue, and 1 tablespoon water and brush over the front of each starfish; dust with glitter. Let dry. Repeat for the back of the pieces.

3. Arrange painted starfish on the wreath form and use hot glue to secure. Loop the ribbon around the top for hanging.

PERFECT POINSETTIAS

Make room for crepe paper poinsettias that will bloom year after year. Arrange the paper bracts around a bundle of glittered berries.

WHAT YOU NEED (FOR ONE POINSETTIA)

Roll of 19½-inch-wide heavyweight crepe paper in ivory and metallic gold (See Sources, page 160) • 24-gauge cloth-covered white florists wire • Wired artificial glittered berries • Crafts glue • Small paintbrush • White florists tape

WHAT YOU DO

MAKE THE BRACTS AND LEAVES

1. Enlarge and trace bract and leaf patterns, right, onto white paper; cut out. Unroll ivory crepe paper, noting direction of the ridges that run the length of the paper. Place a bract pattern on the crepe paper so a ridge runs through the center of the pattern; trace and cut out. Repeat with each pattern to cut two or three small bracts, two or three medium bracts, and five or six large bracts. In the same manner, cut two or three leaves from metallic gold crepe paper.

2. From florists wire, cut a 5-inch length for each small bract, a 6-inch length for each medium bract, and a 7-inch length for each large bract and each leaf. Run a line of glue along the ridge on the back of a bract and adhere appropriate wire on the glue line, placing the wire end approximately ¼ inch from the bract tip. Repeat for each bract and leaf. Let dry.

3. Gently fold each bract and leaf in half along the wire with wrong sides together. Gently pull on the edges of each piece to create a slightly ruffled effect. Twist bottom edges around wire stems.

ASSEMBLE THE FLOWER

1. Gather berry wires together and wrap white florists tape around the wires. Place small and medium bracts around berries, then place large bracts behind the small and medium bracts; secure with florists tape. Add leaves behind the bracts and wrap tape around all wires. **Note:** If flower becomes too top heavy, add a length of wire to the wire bundle and cover with florists tape.

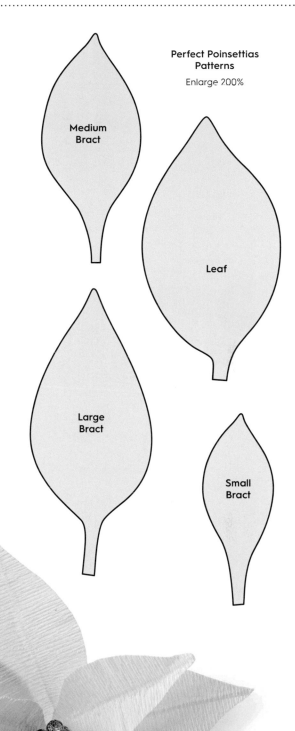

Perfect Poinsettias Patterns

Enlarge 200%

Medium Bract

Leaf

Large Bract

Small Bract

SHOW YOUR STRIPES

Plain wood balls are transformed into shimmering ornaments with a little white paint and color accents.

WHAT YOU NEED
Wooden balls in three sizes: 1½ inches, 2 inches, and 2½ inches in diameter • Painters tape • Small paintbrush • White acrylic paint • Crafts glue • Fine white glitter • ⅛-inch-wide and ¹⁄₁₆-inch-wide fingernail striping tape in metallic silver and metallic gold • Hot-glue gun and glue sticks • 2-inch-long gold and silver tassels • Small screw eyes • White and gold bakers twine

WHAT YOU DO
1. Apply painters tape as desired around wooden balls to mask off areas. Paint exposed areas white; let dry.
2. Brush painted areas with a thin coat of diluted crafts glue. Sprinkle wet glue with white glitter and shake off excess; let dry. Remove painters tape.
3. Apply fingernail striping tape as desired around the balls to create stripes.
4. Hot-glue a tassel to the bottom of an ornament if desired. Screw a screw eye into the top of each ornament. Thread a short length of bakers twine through each screw eye and tie the ends in a knot to create a hanging loop.

SNOWTIME SNOWFLAKES

Folded rice paper is the perfect lightweight paper to use for holiday snowflakes. Embellish with faux crystals for shimmering touches.

WHAT YOU NEED

Roll of rice paper • Heavy-duty spray starch • Iridescent shimmer spray, glitter, or sequins • Iron

WHAT YOU NEED (FOR ONE SNOWFLAKE)

1. Cut a square of desired size from rice paper. Referring to the Snowflake Folding Diagrams, below, fold the paper square into a triangle.

2. Cut out the notches and shapes along the curves through all folded layers. Remove the small pieces and unfold the paper triangle to reveal the snowflake.

3. Spray snowflake with starch and gently press with a warm, dry iron. Embellish snowflake as desired with iridescent shimmer spray, glitter, or sequins.

Snowflake Folding Diagrams

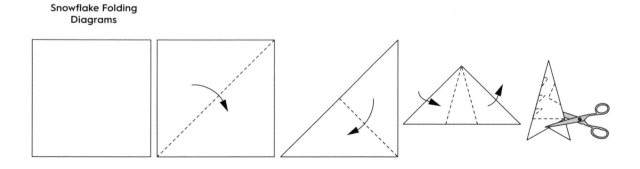

BRANCHES AND BLOSSOMS

A low wood bowl serves as a festive centerpiece. Set a water-tight container into a decorative bowl. Fit hydrated floral foam in the container. Add carnation and chrysanthemum stems into the foam. Tuck in bits of greenery and pinecones. Finish with a purchased candle. Never leave a burning candle unattended.

CHRISTMAS CARD CENTERPIECE

Last year's pretty white Christmas cards are cut and centered on a square glass vase to make a sweet and sentimental centerpiece. Cut the front from the cards and center on each side of the square vase using double-stick tape to hold in place. Wrap a pretty ribbon around the vase and tie in a knot. Fill the vase with white flowers and holiday greenery.

CUSTOM TAGS

Last year's Christmas cards in shades of white are transformed into custom gift tags with a snip of the scissors and a touch of glitter.

WHAT YOU NEED

White Christmas cards • Scissors • Crafts glue • Fine white glitter • Paper punch • Fine ribbon

WHAT YOU DO

1. Choose cards that have small motifs that can be embellished. Trim the cards to the size of a gift tag.
2. Add dots and lines of crafts glue on areas of the card that can be embellished, such as around tree lines, hats, mittens, etc. Sprinkle with glitter. Let dry.
3. Punch a hole in the corner of the tag and thread the ribbon through the hole to tie on the package.

SNOWY LUMINARIAS

Add plenty of shimmer to your holiday with luminarias made from humble canning jars dressed up with lots of sparkle.

WHAT YOU NEED

Canning jars in desired size • Epsom salt • White glitter • Crafts glue • Water • Paintbrush • Parchment paper • Twine • Small jingle bells • Bits of greenery

WHAT YOU DO

1. Be sure the jars are clean and dry. In a large bowl mix equal parts of Epsom salt and white glitter.

2. In a small bowl make a mixture of 3 parts glue to 1 part water. Use a paintbrush to paint a thin layer of the mixture onto the jar.

3. Roll the jar into the mixture until it is covered. Set on parchment paper to dry.

4. Embellish the jar with twine, jingle bells, and bits of greenery. Place a tea candle or votive candle in the jar.

Never leave a burning candle unattended.

Let It Snow!

Sprinkles of sugar work wintertime magic to give Christmas cookies a festive finish sure to delight.

CHERRY WALNUT BALLS

There's nothing like a fresh coating of snow. Retoss these buttery balls in powdered sugar just before serving and add a sprinkling of edible glitter.

WHAT YOU NEED

1   cup butter, softened
½   cup powdered sugar
½   tsp. almond extract
½   tsp. vanilla
2   cups all-purpose flour
¾   cup chopped walnuts, toasted
¼   cup coarsely chopped maraschino cherries, drained
     and patted very dry
     Powdered sugar
     Red edible glitter* (optional)

WHAT YOU DO

1. Preheat oven to 325°F. In a large bowl beat butter with a mixer on medium 30 seconds. Add the ½ cup powdered sugar, the almond extract, and vanilla. Beat until combined, scraping bowl as needed. Beat in flour. Stir in walnuts and cherries.
2. Shape dough into 1-inch balls; place 2 inches apart on ungreased cookie sheets. Bake 18 to 20 minutes or until bottoms are light brown. Cool on cookie sheets 5 minutes.
3. Roll warm cookies in powdered sugar; cool on a wire rack. If desired, roll again in powdered sugar and, if desired, sprinkle with edible glitter before serving. Makes about 48 balls.
*Tip Look for edible glitter in the cake-decorating department of hobby and crafts stores.

SNOWFLAKE SANDWICHES

Make these sandwich cookies sparkle with a bright-color jam and cover the top cookies with powdered sugar before assembling.

WHAT YOU NEED

½   cup butter, softened
½   cup butter-flavor shortening
1   cup granulated sugar
2   tsp. lemon zest
¾   tsp. baking powder
¼   tsp. baking soda
     Dash salt
1   egg
⅓   cup sour cream
1   tsp. vanilla
2¾ cups all-purpose flour
1   cup jam or jelly
     Powdered sugar

WHAT YOU DO

1. In a large bowl beat butter and shortening with a mixer on medium 30 seconds. Add next five ingredients (through salt). Beat until combined, scraping bowl as needed. Beat in egg, sour cream, and vanilla. Beat in flour. Divide dough in half. Cover and chill until easy to handle (about 2 hours).

2. Preheat oven to 375°F. On a lightly floured surface roll dough, one portion at a time, to ⅛ inch thick. Using a 2½- to 3-inch snowflake-shape cookie cutter, cut out dough. Using a 1-inch desired-shape cookie cutter, cut and remove shapes from centers of half the cookies. Place cookies 1 inch apart on an ungreased cookie sheet.
3. Bake 7 to 8 minutes or until edges are firm and bottoms are very light brown. Cool on cookie sheet 1 minute. Remove; cool on a wire rack.
4. Spread jam onto bottoms of cookies without cutouts. Generously sprinkle cookies with cutouts with powdered sugar. Top jam with cutout cookies, powdered sugar side up, to make sandwiches. Makes about 40 sandwiches.

ALMOND WREATHS

Granulated or coarse sugar, instead of powdered sugar, gives these festive cookies a shimmering, icy look and crunchy texture.

WHAT YOU NEED
1   lb. crumbled almond paste
⅔   cup granulated sugar
½   tsp. salt
3   egg whites, lightly beaten
½   cup all-purpose flour
1   cup sliced almonds
    Granulated or coarse sugar

WHAT YOU DO
1. Preheat oven to 350°F. Line cookie sheets with parchment paper. In a large bowl beat almond paste, the ⅔ cup sugar, the salt, and two of the egg whites until a thick paste forms. Sprinkle flour over work surface. Transfer paste to surface; knead into flour until a smooth dough forms. Roll to ½ inch thick.
2. Using a floured donut cutter, cut dough into 24 wreaths, rerolling dough as necessary. Arrange wreaths 1 inch apart on prepared cookie sheets. Brush with some of the remaining egg white. Decorate with almond slices. Brush again with egg white. Sprinkle with granulated or coarse sugar. Bake 16 to 18 minutes or until golden brown. Cool on a wire rack. Makes 24 wreaths.

CHOCOLATE CRINKLES

Pristine powdered sugar-coated dough balls burst in the oven into melt-in-your mouth cocoa-flavor crinkle cookies. No need to redust—you want those cracks amid the melty sugar coating.

WHAT YOU NEEDS
4   oz. unsweetened chocolate
½   cup shortening
3   eggs, lightly beaten
2   cups granulated sugar
2   tsp. baking powder
2   tsp. vanilla
¼   tsp. salt
2   cups all-purpose flour
⅔   cup powdered sugar

WHAT YOU DO
1. In a small saucepan combine chocolate and shortening. Heat and stir over low until melted and smooth. Cool 15 minutes.
2. In a large bowl combine eggs, granulated sugar, baking powder, vanilla, and salt. Stir in chocolate mixture. Gradually add flour, stirring until thoroughly combined. Cover dough; chill about 2 hours or until easy to handle.
3. Preheat oven to 375°F. Lightly grease cookie sheets. Shape dough into 1-inch balls; roll in powdered sugar to generously coat. Place balls 2 inches apart on prepared cookie sheets. Bake about 10 minutes or until edges are just set. Cool on a wire rack. Makes 60 cookies.
To Store Layer cookies between sheets of waxed paper in an airtight container; cover. Store at room temperature up to 3 days or freeze up to 3 months.

COCONUT SPRITZ

A pastry bag with a star tip simplifies the creation of these scalloped cookies. A special spritz cookie press is not required.

WHAT YOU NEED

2	cups unsalted butter, softened
1	cup granulated sugar
2	eggs
½	cup unsweetened coconut milk
3½	cups all-purpose flour
1	cup sweetened shredded coconut, finely chopped in a food processor
1	tsp. salt
½	tsp. baking powder
	Powdered sugar (optional)

WHAT YOU DO

1. Preheat oven to 325°F. Line cookie sheets with parchment paper. Trace 2½-inch circles 1 inch apart on paper; flip over.
2. In a large bowl beat butter and granulated sugar with a mixer on medium until light and fluffy. Add eggs, one at a time, beating on low after each addition. Beat in coconut milk. In a medium bowl whisk together flour, coconut, salt, and baking powder. Add to egg mixture; beat on low until combined.
3. Transfer batter to a pastry bag fitted with a ¼-inch star tip. Pipe in small loops to form a circle, using drawn circle as a guide. Bake 10 to 12 minutes or until edges just begin to brown. Cool completely on cookie sheets on a wire rack. If desired, sprinkle with powdered sugar. Makes about 70 cookies.
Cookie Tree Trace circles in graduated sizes from 1 inch to 6 inches. Prepare as directed, baking larger cookies 2 to 4 minutes longer. Stack from largest to smallest to create tree. Sprinkle with powdered sugar and, if desired, top with a decorative candy.

BLOOD ORANGE BARS

Give these citrusy bars a snowy look with snowflake cutouts. Lay a cutout on each bar and shake on powdered sugar through a fine-mesh sieve. Carefully remove the cutouts.

WHAT YOU NEED

1	cup all-purpose flour
3	Tbsp. powdered sugar
¼	tsp. salt
⅓	cup cold butter, cut up
1	cup granulated sugar
2	eggs
2	tsp. blood orange zest or orange zest
⅔	cup fresh blood orange juice or orange juice
2	drops red food coloring (optional)
2	Tbsp. all-purpose flour
¼	tsp. salt
	Powdered sugar

WHAT YOU DO

1. Preheat oven to 350°F. Line an 8-inch square pan with foil, extending foil over edges of pan. Grease foil.
2. For crust, in a large bowl stir together the 1 cup flour, the 3 Tbsp. powdered sugar, and the ¼ tsp. salt. Using a pastry blender, cut in butter until mixture resembles coarse crumbs. Press crumb mixture evenly and firmly into bottom of prepared pan. Bake about 15 minutes or until light golden around edges.
3. In a medium bowl whisk together the granulated sugar, eggs, orange zest, orange juice, and, if desired, food coloring until smooth. Stir in the 2 Tbsp. flour and remaining ¼ tsp. salt. Pour orange mixture over hot crust.
4. Bake 20 to 25 minutes more or until set. Cool completely in pan on a wire rack. Use foil to lift uncut bars out of pan. Cut into bars. Dust bars with powdered sugar. Makes 16 bars.
To Store Place bars in a single layer in an airtight container; cover. Store in the refrigerator up to 3 days.

molasses. Beat in as much of the flour mixture as you can with the mixer. Stir in any remaining flour mixture.

3. Shape dough into 2-inch balls using ¼ cup dough per cookie. Roll balls in the coarse sugar and place 2½ inches apart on an ungreased cookie sheet.

4. Bake 11 to 13 minutes or until cookies are light brown and puffed. (Do not overbake or cookies will not be chewy.) Cool on cookie sheet 2 minutes. Remove; cool on wire racks. Makes 24 cookies.

Mini Ginger Cookies Prepare as directed, except shape dough into 1-inch balls. Place 1½ inches apart on ungreased cookie sheets. Bake in a 350°F oven 8 to 9 minutes or until cookies are light brown and puffed. (Do not overbake or cookies will not be chewy.) Cool on cookie sheets 1 minute. Remove; cool on wire racks. Makes about 120 cookies.

COCONUT-PECAN SNOWBALLS

These are your classic snowball cookies (sometimes called Mexican Wedding Cookies)—with a little coconut added to the mix. (Pictured on pages 122–123.)

WHAT YOU NEED

1	cup butter, softened
½	cup powdered sugar
1	Tbsp. water
1	tsp. vanilla
2	cups all-purpose flour
¾	cup finely chopped pecans, toasted (tip, page 34)
¾	cup finely chopped coconut
¾	cup powdered sugar

WHAT YOU DO

1. In a large bowl beat butter with a mixer on medium 30 seconds. Add ½ cup powdered sugar. Beat until combined, scraping bowl as needed. Beat in the water and vanilla until combined. Beat in as much of the flour as you can with the mixer. Stir in any remaining flour, the pecans, and coconut. Cover and chill 30 to 60 minutes or until dough is easy to handle.

2. Preheat oven to 325°F. Shape dough into 1-inch balls. Place balls 1 inch apart on ungreased cookie sheets. Bake about 15 minutes or until bottoms are light brown. Remove; cool on wire racks.

3. Place ¾ cup powdered sugar in a large plastic bag. Add cooled cookies, a few at a time, shaking gently to coat. (Or use a fine-mesh sieve to lightly dust cookies with powdered sugar.) Makes 36 cookies.

Cocoa-Covered Snowballs Prepare as directed, except in Step 3 reduce the powdered sugar to ½ cup and stir in 3 Tbsp. unsweetened cocoa powder. Shake cooled cookies in the cocoa mixture.

BIG GINGER COOKIES

If you don't have coarse sugar to give these nicely spiced cookies some sparkle, regular granulated sugar will do the trick equally well.

WHAT YOU NEED

4½	cups all-purpose flour
4	tsp. ground ginger
2	tsp. baking soda
1½	tsp. ground cinnamon
1	tsp. ground cloves
¼	tsp. salt
1½	cups shortening
2	cups granulated sugar
2	eggs
½	cup molasses
¾	cup coarse sugar or granulated sugar

WHAT YOU DO

1. Preheat oven to 350°F. In a medium bowl stir together first six ingredients (through salt).

2. In a large bowl beat shortening with a mixer on low 30 seconds. Gradually add 2 cups granulated sugar. Beat until combined, scraping bowl as needed. Beat in eggs and

MATCHA-GINGER SNOWBALLS

Matcha! Lately, bright-green matcha tea has lit the culinary world on fire, showing up in everything from ice cream to pancakes. Part of its draw is the super-high level of antioxidants that come from directly consuming the ground leaves (versus infusing the tea leaves in water, then discarding them, as with traditional tea). As a bonus, the tea is such a vivid hue, it dyes food a naturally festive green for the holidays.

WHAT YOU NEED

½   cup shortening
1   Tbsp. grated fresh ginger or 2 tsp. ground ginger
1   Tbsp. vanilla
1   Tbsp. matcha (green tea powder)
1   tsp. lemon zest
1   cup packed brown sugar
1   tsp. baking powder
½   tsp. baking soda
¼   tsp. salt
2   eggs
2½ cups all-purpose flour
    Green food coloring (optional)
1   recipe Powdered Sugar Glaze
    White nonpareils

WHAT YOU DO

1. In a large bowl beat shortening, ginger, vanilla, matcha, and lemon zest with a mixer on medium until combined. Add brown sugar; beat until fluffy. Beat in baking powder, baking soda, and salt. Beat in eggs. Beat in flour. If desired, beat in green food coloring. Chill dough 1 hour or until easy to handle.
2. Preheat oven to 350°F. Shape dough into 1-inch balls. Place balls 2 inches apart on ungreased cookie sheets. Bake 10 to 12 minutes or until lightly browned. Cool on cookie sheets 2 minutes. Remove; cool on wire racks.
3. Dip tops in Powdered Sugar Glaze, letting excess drip off; sprinkle with nonpareils. Place cookies on waxed paper and let set. Makes 48 cookies.
Powdered Sugar Glaze In a bowl stir together 1½ cups powdered sugar and 1 to 2 Tbsp. water to make the glaze a thick coating consistency.

STAR ANISE CRESCENTS

These moon-shape cookies are flavored with a different kind of spice than the traditional Christmas spice cookie—Chinese five-spice powder.

WHAT YOU NEED

1	vanilla bean, split lengthwise
2	cups powdered sugar
⅛	tsp. five-spice powder
1½	cups butter, softened
½	cup granulated sugar
2	cups slivered almonds, finely ground
½	tsp. salt
3	cups all-purpose flour

WHAT YOU DO

1. Using the tip of a small sharp knife, scrape out the seeds from the vanilla bean. In a food processor process the vanilla seeds, powdered sugar, and five-spice powder until vanilla seeds are well incorporated.

2. In a large bowl beat butter with a mixer on medium to high 30 seconds. Add the granulated sugar, almonds, and salt. Beat until combined, scraping bowl occasionally. Beat in as much of the flour as you can with the mixer. Stir in any remaining flour. Cover and chill dough about 1 hour or until easy to handle.

3. Preheat oven to 350°F. Lightly grease cookie sheets. Shape dough into 1-inch balls, then mold each ball into a crescent shape. Place crescents 2 inches apart on the prepared cookie sheets.

4. Bake 8 to 10 minutes or until set and edges are golden. Cool on cookie sheets 5 minutes. While cookies are warm, roll them in powdered sugar mixture. Cool on a wire rack. Roll cooled cookies in the powdered sugar mixture again. Makes 48 cookies.

To Make Ahead Prepare and shape dough. Place crescents on parchment- or foil-lined cookie sheets; freeze. Transfer frozen crescents to a covered airtight container. Freeze up to 3 months. To bake, arrange frozen crescents on cookie sheets. Let stand at room temperature while the oven preheats. Bake 10 to 12 minutes or until cookies are set and edges are golden.

KEY LIME COINS

It's snowing in the tropics! A dusting of powdered sugar gives these citrusy cookies a touch of winter in the Northland.

WHAT YOU NEED

¾	cup butter, softened
⅓	cup powdered sugar
1	tsp. lime zest
2	Tbsp. Key lime juice or lime juice
1	Tbsp. water
1	tsp. vanilla
1¾	cups all-purpose flour
2	Tbsp. cornstarch
½	tsp. salt
2	cups powdered sugar

WHAT YOU DO

1. In a large bowl beat butter with a mixer on medium to high 30 seconds. Add the next five ingredients (through vanilla). Beat until combined, scraping bowl as needed. Beat in the flour, cornstarch, and salt.

2. Divide dough in half. Shape each half into a 10-inch-long roll; wrap rolls in plastic wrap. Chill at least 3 hours or up to 2 days.

3. Preheat oven to 325°F. Line cookie sheets with parchment paper. Using a sharp, thin-bladed knife, cut rolls crosswise into ¼-inch slices. Place slices 2 inches apart on the prepared cookie sheets.

4. Bake 15 to 18 minutes or just until bottoms are golden. Cool on cookie sheets 4 minutes. Place the 2 cups powdered sugar in a large bowl. Gently toss warm cookies, two or three at a time, in powdered sugar. Cool on a wire rack. Makes 80 cookies.

LEMONY STAR SANDWICHES

A filling of mascarpone cheese, butter, lemon curd, and powdered sugar keeps the tops and bottoms of these stellar cookies together.

WHAT YOU NEED

½	cup butter, softened
½	cup butter-flavor shortening
1	cup granulated sugar
2	tsp. lemon zest
¾	tsp. baking powder
¼	tsp. baking soda
	Dash salt
⅓	cup sour cream
1	egg
1	tsp. vanilla
2¾	cups all-purpose flour
1	recipe Creamy Lemon Filling
	Powdered sugar

WHAT YOU DO

1. In a large bowl beat butter and shortening with a mixer on medium to high 30 seconds. Add the next five ingredients (through salt). Beat until combined, scraping bowl occasionally. Beat in sour cream, egg, and vanilla. Beat in as much of the flour as you can with the mixer. Stir in any remaining flour. Divide dough in half. Cover and chill dough about 2 hours or until easy to handle.

2. Preheat oven to 375°F. On a floured surface roll half the dough at a time until ⅛ inch thick. Using a 2½- to 3-inch star-shape cookie cutter, cut out dough. Using a 1-inch star-shape cookie cutter, cut a star from the center of half of the cookies. Place cookies 1 inch apart on ungreased cookie sheets.

3. Bake 7 to 8 minutes or until edges are firm and bottoms are very light brown. Cool on cookie sheets 1 minute. Remove; cool on wire rack.

4. Just before serving, spread about 1 tsp. of Creamy Lemon Filling over flat sides (bottoms) of cookies without cutouts. Press the flat sides of the cookies with cutouts on top of the

cookies with the filling. Generously sprinkle powdered sugar over the cookies. Makes 40 sandwich cookies.

Creamy Lemon Filling In a small bowl beat ⅓ cup mascarpone cheese or 3 oz. softened cream cheese and 1 Tbsp. softened butter with a mixer on medium to high 30 seconds. Beat in ¼ cup lemon curd until combined. Gradually add 1 cup powdered sugar, beating on medium until smooth and creamy. Store in refrigerator until needed.

To Store Layer unfilled cookies between sheets of waxed paper in an airtight container; cover. Store in the refrigerator up to 3 days or freeze up to 3 months. Thaw if frozen. Fill cookies with Creamy Lemon Filling and sprinkle with powdered sugar just before serving.

Plentiful Pinecones

Give the humble pinecone a fresh and modern update with projects and DIY ideas for every corner of your holiday home.

NATURAL COTTON AND PINECONE WREATH

A pretty pinecone wreath is softened for the holidays with little balls of natural cotton added between the textured pinecones. Choose a purchased pinecone wreath available at crafts stores or make your own—then tuck in the cotton bolls and little sticks.

PINECONE FOREST

Slender pinecones stand together on little slices of wood to make a lovely forest for your holiday mantel or table.

WHAT YOU NEED

Sliced pieces of wood (available at most crafts stores)
• Pinecones • Small wooden dowels cut to desired size
• Drill and drill bit the same size as the wooden dowel
• Hot-glue gun and glue stick • Small strips of torn fabric

WHAT YOU NEED

1. For each tall tree, mark the center of a sliced piece of wood and drill into the center of the slice. Insert the dowel into the hole, securing with a small dab of hot glue. Drill into the bottom center of the pinecone. Insert dowel into hole in pinecone, securing with a small dab of hot glue. Embellish the dowel trunk with torn pieces of fabric.
2. For the short trees, use hot glue to glue the pinecones directly to the wood slices.
3. Arrange the trees to represent a forest.

Make your holiday a little lighter and brighter with whitewashed pinecones and birch wood. Create this lovely tree in an evening and keep it for years to come. Make plenty of these beautiful pinecones to have on hand for other crafts projects.

WHITEWASHED BEAUTY

Various sizes of whitewashed pinecones cluster together to make for a lavish tree centerpiece.

WHAT YOU NEED

4×9-inch foam cone such as Styrofoam • 30 whitewashed pinecones (see instructions, below) • Hot-glue gun and low-melt glue sticks • Metal floor flange with ¾-inch opening • 1×8-inch slice of birch • ¾×9-inch piece of birch • Paring knife

HOW TO MAKE WHITEWASH PINECONES:

In a large bowl mix 1 cup white paint and 4 cups water. Soak the cones for 15 minutes in the paint mixture. Drip dry and do not rinse. When almost dry to the touch, bake at 180°F for 1 to 3 hours. Set on parchment paper to dry.

WHAT YOU DO

1. To make the base of the tree, center and screw the metal floor flange to the 1×8-inch piece of birch. Glue the other piece of birch securely into the flange.
2. Using the paring knife, cut a channel into the foam cone to later insert 3 or 4 inches of the birch-pole trunk.
3. Choose the pinecones you want to use for your tree from the whitewashed ones you have made. Starting at the top of the tree, use hot glue to glue the dry cones in rows. Continue until the foam cone is covered.
4. Add glue to the trunk and push in place.

MAGICAL HOLIDAY GNOMES

Even though this grouping of happy gnomes looks alike, each of these little fellows has its own special personality.

WHAT YOU NEED (FOR ONE GNOME)

Pinecone • Red felt • ¾-inch wood ball (available at crafts stores) • Tan yarn • Hot-glue gun and glue sticks

WHAT YOU DO

1. Copy or trace the pattern, right, and cut out. Cut the hat shape from red felt. Fold the edges around to form a cone and secure with hot glue. Set aside.
2. Make a pom-pom from tan yarn for the beard. (See "How to Make a Pom-Pom" on page 79). Set aside.
3. Use hot glue to attach the pom-pom to the pinecone. Use hot glue to attach hat to the pom-pom and the bead in the middle for the nose.

Magical Holiday Gnomes
Hat Template

GRACED WITH GARLAND

While you're wiring clusters for a garland, make extras to use as decor such as package tie-ons and in floral arrangements.

WHAT YOU NEED

5-foot length of heavy twine (for a 4-foot garland)
● 80 pinecones ● Green florists wire ● Wire cutters ● Ribbon

WHAT YOU DO

1. Start by making a large hanging loop at each end of the twine. Twist a 7-inch length of wire tightly around the base of each pinecone, leaving about 3 inches of wire loose.
2. Create clusters of three or four pinecones by twisting together the wires. Fill the twine with wired-on clusters of pinecones. Add ribbon bows to the ends and hang.

SNOWFLAKE SYMMETRY

In nature, no two snowflakes are identical. With pinecones, the same is quite possibly true. Create these one-of-a-kind beauties from whitewashed pinecones.

WHAT YOU NEED

One large whitewashed pinecone (see "How to Whitewash Pinecones," page 138) • 24 (approximately) smaller whitewashed pinecones • 2-inch cardboard square • 6 wooden skewers cut into 5-inch lengths • Hot-glue gun and glue sticks

WHAT YOU DO

1. For a guide, draw a circle divided into six equal pie-shape segments on the cardboard. Position the skewer lengths over the drawn lines.

2. Using hot glue, secure the skewers to the cardboard center. Turn the skewer form over. Hot-glue the large pinecone to the center; hot-glue the smaller pinecones along the skewer lengths. Trim away excess skewer.

SPARKLING PINECONES

Dress up natural pinecones with a dusting of glitter for some holiday sparkle. Use a paintbrush and crafts glue to paint the bracts and then dust with glitter. Let dry and arrange with fresh greenery and matte-finish ornaments for a lovely centerpiece.

OMBRE-TIPPED WREATH

Subtle color changes make this pinecone wreath a pretty little work of art.

WHAT YOU NEED
Pinecones • Crafts paint in desired shades of color • Foam paint brush • Flat wreath form • Hot-glue gun and glue sticks

WHAT YOU DO
1. Plan the colors of the wreath by choosing or mixing paints from light to dark in desired colors.
2. Paint the tips of the pinecones using a foam brush and crafts paint, starting with light at the top and dark at bottom. Let dry.
3. Attach to wreath form using hot glue. Let dry. Loop twine at the top for hanging.

ARTFUL PINECONE GARLAND

Little pieces of felt are layered on a simple length of string to make a naturally beautiful garland for tree or mantel.

WHAT YOU NEED
Nonwoven felt such as National Nonwovens in various shades of brown, tan, and peach • Scissors • Hot-glue gun and glue sticks • String or yarn

WHAT YOU DO
1. Copy or trace the template, right, and cut out. Set aside.
2. Cut 1×1-inch squares from various colors of felt. Cut in half to form triangles. Using the template as a guide, lay the triangles down, starting at the bottom of the template. Attach where pieces intersect each other using hot glue.
3. Lay the pinecones shapes on the string and glue in place.

Artful Pinecone Garland
Template

STAR LIGHT, STAR BRIGHT

In the same easy manner you drew a Christmas star as a child, you can build one using wood lattice and pretty little pinecones.

WHAT YOU NEED

Five 22-inch lengths of ½-inch wood lattice ● #8 screws ● Screwdriver ● Hot-glue gun and glue sticks ● 3-inch pinecones (approximately 72) ● Scissors ● Tan felt

WHAT YOU DO

1. Crisscross the pieces of lattice and secure with screws. Cut 1-inch felt circles from tan felt and hot-glue to the bottom of each pinecone. (This ensures a better bond to the wood.)

2. Arrange and hot-glue the pinecones in place. If desired, cover both sides of the form to suspend it in a window or to use as a tree topper.

SNOW-TIPPED CHRISTMAS TREES

Pinecones painted with white paint line up on large wood dowels to create a simple and stunning centerpiece.

WHAT YOU NEED

Wood kabob skewers • Saw • ⅛-inch hardware nut • White paint • Paintbrush • Pinecones with flat bottoms • Wood doll-head knobs available at crafts stores • Drill • Drill bit • Hot-glue gun and glue sticks

WHAT YOU DO

1. Cut the wooden skewers to 2- to 4-inch lengths. Push one end of the skewer firmly into an ⅛-inch hardware nut until even with the nut edge. Secure with hot glue. Set aside.

2. Choose a variety of pinecones with flat bottoms or cut away the stems so they sit flat. Paint with white paint. Let dry.

3. Center and glue a nut and skewer to the bottom of each cone. For tree bases, drill the existing hole of the dollhead knobs all the way through using an ⅛-inch bit. Paint white and let dry.

4. Stand the base on its flat bottom and insert the tree-trunk skewer into the hole, using hot glue to secure.

SEASONAL SWAGGER

As easy as gather and tie, this elegant swag can be made in no time. Layer favorite greenery and wire with green florists wire. Wire pinecones to the top of the swag. Make a double bow of gold and white ribbon and wire to the top.

Please
Be Seated

Create Christmas place settings that are
sure to bring them to the table with merry
smiles and happy anticipation.

Miss Maddie Lyn

MINI-GIFT NAPKIN RINGS
Simple cardstock paper quickly transforms into tiny
presents that wrap around each guest napkin.

WHAT YOU NEED
Patterned cardstock • Scissors • Hot-glue gun and glue
sticks • Crafts knife such as Xacto knife • Ruler • Mat board
(optional) • Narrow ribbon

WHAT YOU DO
1. Cut the patterned cardstock into a 7½×1-inch piece. Using
a ruler and scissors or crafts knife, score the paper every
1½ inches.
2. Fold the paper into a box shape, overlapping ends. Secure
with hot glue.
3. Wrap the box with ribbon and add a ribbon bow, securing
with hot glue.
4. Slide the napkin into the napkin ring.

Napkin Folding Diagrams

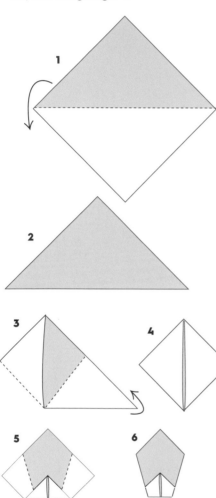

TAILORED SOPHISTICATE

This silvery gray table setting answers the call for a modern table; a touch of deep red adds richness and warmth. A bowl of sugared fruit (with dusty miller leaves tucked in) supplies the sparkle.

TO MAKE THE POUCH-STYLE FOLDED NAPKIN
1. Place a cloth napkin diagonally on a flat work surface, diagram 1. (Use an oversize napkin so that when it's folded it will be taller than the silverware. Our napkin is 22×21 inches.) Fold the bottom point up to the top point, creating a triangle, diagram 2. Fold the left and then the right corners up to the top, diagram 3, creating a diamond shape, diagram 4.
2. Turn the napkin over. Fold the bottom one-third of the napkin upward and then fold the left and right sides underneath the napkin, diagram 5. This will create a pouch in front, diagram 6.
3. Print the word "Noel" and cut out. Make a small banner shape from silver cardstock. Glue the "Noel" piece to the banner. Glue the banner to a piece of velvet ribbon and tie the ribbon in back of the napkin. Place silverware in the pouch.

CHRISTMAS BELLS

Bring some jingle to the table with napkin rings created using printed fabric and jingle bells.

WHAT YOU NEED (FOR ONE NAPKIN HOLDER)
Cardboard paper tube (from paper towels) • Scissors • Print fabric • Crafts glue • Rickrack • Jingle bell • Bakers twine

WHAT YOU DO
1. Cut the paper tube to measure 2 inches. Cut a 2½×6-inch piece of fabric.
2. Use crafts glue to glue the rickrack to both sides of the paper tube, making sure that the edge of the rick rack shows. Let dry.
3. Use an iron to press ¼ inch under on the long sides of the fabric. Glue the fabric on to the tube, over the rick rack. Trim edges
4. Thread the jingle bell on the twine and tie around the napkin holder. Slide the napkin into the holder.

POM-POMS PLACE SETTING

Pom-poms encircle a plain white plate for a fun-to-share place setting.

WHAT YOU NEED

- White plate for charger • Clear plate • Red pom-pom trim
- Scissors • Masking tape • Chalkboard

WHAT YOU DO

1. Be sure the plate is clean and dry. Cut enough of the pompom trim to fit around the perimeter of the white plate or charger. Tape the edge of the trim under the plate with just the pom-poms showing.

2. Lay the clear plate on top of the charger. Place a polka-dot or striped napkin on the plate. Add a name tag. Set place setting on a chalkboard.

St. Nick Napkin Rings Templates

Enlarge 150%

Santa Wrap Template

Santa Mustache Template

Cut 2

Santa Face Template

ST. NICK NAPKIN RINGS

Santa will be the most popular guest at your table when he appears at each place setting.

WHAT YOU NEED
- White cardstock • Beige cardstock • Red pom-poms
- White napkin ring form • Black marker • Hot-glue gun and glue sticks • Foam adhesive dot • Scissors

WHAT YOU DO
1. Enlarge and copy or trace template shapes, above. Cut the following shapes from cardstock: Santa wrap and Santa mustache from white, Santa face from beige.
2. Wrap face around the napkin ring form, securing with hot glue. Draw two eyes on the face using a marker; attach with hot glue. Attach mustache using foam adhesive dots. Attach pom-pom with hot glue.
3. Slide napkin into holder.

PRAIRIE TABLE SETTING

Pewter plates and fresh plums make for a warmly wonderful holiday table setting. Start with a place mat trimmed with rickrack. Then add gray or pewter plates and charger. Tie on fresh greenery and a name card tucked with a sprig of evergreen. A vintage muffin tin holds votive candles.

FASHION PLATES

Metallics mix with black and white as naturally as old mixes with new. Pair silver goblets with bamboo-style flatware and silver and gold chargers. Hints of soft pink tie the holiday palette together.

TABLETOP ETIQUETTE

Use this guide (and the illustration, right) to ensure that your holiday table is perfectly set.

DINNER PLATE
Place this large plate directly on the table in the absence of a charger.

SALAD PLATE
Set the salad plate atop the dinner plate. It should be removed after the salad course is eaten.

SOUP BOWL
If soup is being served, place the bowl on the salad plate.

BREAD PLATE
Place this small plate, slightly larger than a saucer, above and to the left of the dinner plate (directly above the forks).

DINNER FORK
Set the large dinner fork to the immediate left of the dinner plate.

SALAD FORK
Because the salad fork is used first, place it on the outside—to the left of the dinner fork.

DINNER KNIFE
The dinner knife goes to the immediate right of the dinner plate, with the blade facing inward.

TEASPOON
Place the teaspoon to the right of the dinner knife, with the bowl facing up.

SOUP SPOON
If soup is being served, the soup spoon should sit to the right of the teaspoon.

DINNER NAPKIN
Place the dinner napkin to the left of the salad fork. For a more casual presentation (or if you're not using a soup bowl), place it on the salad plate.

WATER GLASS
Place this glass in easy reach above the dinner plate. Fill it with chilled water before guests are seated.

CHAMPAGNE FLUTE
Situate the champagne flute to the right of the water glass—between it and the and wine glass. The flute's tall and narrow shape keeps the champagne bubbly.

WINE GLASS
Place the wine glass to the right of the champagne flute. A red-wine glass is larger than a white-wine glass; its large bowl allows the wine to breathe.

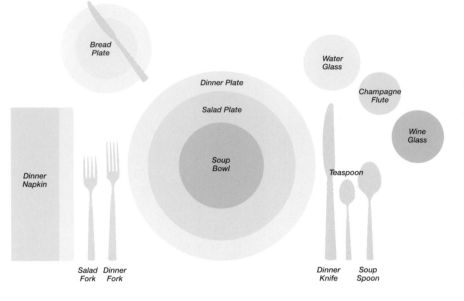

ENTERTAINING TIPS FROM THE PROS

SET IT AND FORGET IT
Set the table up to two days ahead and then cover it with a clean bedsheet to keep the dishes and glasses from gathering dust. This will give you more time on the day of the party to fine-tune the table decorations.

MAKE GLASSWARE SPARKLE
Avoid dusty or spotty surprises from drinking glasses pulled out at the last minute. Run glasses through the dishwasher before setting the table to make them sparkle. Hand-wash delicate items in advance, too.

MEASURE UP
Let the tablecloth drop 12 to 18 inches from the edges of the table. (Use a silence cloth or pad beneath the cloth to protect the table.) Leave 12 inches between place settings. The dinner plate (or charger) and flatware should sit 1 inch from the edge of the table.

LET THE FOOD DO THE TALKING
Avoid using highly scented flowers or candles on the table. They interfere with the aromas and flavors of the food—plus some guests may be sensitive to certain flowers or perfumed candles.

KEEP SIGHT LINES OPEN
Centerpieces should be below eye level of seated guests—and flaming candles above—so diners can talk across the table easily. **Quick Tip:** Freeze candles before lighting them to prevent messy drips.

CHANGE IT UP
Consider serving dessert somewhere other than at the dining table, such as in the living room (in front of a crackling fire) or a four-season sunroom. Guests will be able to move around a bit before the final bites.

STITCH DIAGRAMS

Backstitch

Straight Stitch

Chain Stitch

Whipstitch

French Knot

Buttonhole Stitch

Running Stitch

Fern Stitch

Star Stitch

Stem Stitch

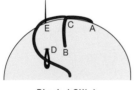

Blanket Stitch

CROCHET ABBREVIATIONS

BEG	begin(ning)
CH	chain
DC	double crochet
HDC	half double crochet
INC	increase
SC	single crochet
SL ST	slip stitch
ST(S	stitch(es)

SOURCES

Crafts Paint
deltacreative.com

Cardstock/Scrapbooking Supplies
hobbylobby.com
michaels.com

Paper Tape/Ribbon
michaels.com

Flower Punch
EKSuccess
amazon.com

Spray Paint
walmart.com
menards.com

Wood Slices/Wood Pieces
michaels.com
Woodcrafter.com

Felt
National Nonwovens
nationalnonwovens.com

Glue
Aleene's Tacky Glue
aleenes.com

Beads
michaels.com
joann.com

Papers and Stickers
memoryboundscrapbook
    store.com
michaels.com
hobbylobby.com

Bakers Twine
hobbylobby.com

Wool Pom-Poms
craftywoolfelt.com

Paper-Wrapped Floral Stems
michaels.com

Ribbon
offray.com

Yarn
yarnspirations.com

CRAFT DESIGNERS

Judy Bailey • Karin Lidbeck-Brent • Lindsay Berger • Jan Carlson • Carol Field Dahlstrom • Roger H. Dahlstrom • Chrissie Grace • Carmen Heffernan • Pam Koelling • Matthew Mead • Janet Pittman • Suzonne Stirling • Jan Temeyer